Macramé
FOR BEGINNERS

Step-By-Step Instructions and High Quality Illustrations for Home and Garden DIY Projects. The Complete Guide for Beginners to Master the Art of Macramé

Lucy Hernández

© **Copyright 2021 by Lucy Hernández - All rights reserved.**

This document is geared towards providing exact and reliable information in regard to the topic and issue covered.

- From a Declaration of Principles which was accepted and approved equally by a Committee of the American Bar Association and a Committee of Publishers and Associations.

In no way is it legal to reproduce, duplicate, or transmit any part of this document in either electronic means or in printed format. All rights reserved.

The information provided herein is stated to be truthful and consistent, in that any liability, in terms of inattention or otherwise, by any usage or abuse of any policies, processes, or directions contained within is the solitary and utter responsibility of the recipient reader. Under no circumstances will any legal responsibility or blame be held against the publisher for any reparation, damages, or monetary loss due to the information herein, either directly or indirectly.

Respective authors own all copyrights not held by the publisher.

The information herein is offered for informational purposes solely and is universal as so. The presentation of the information is without a or any type of guarantee assurance.

The trademarks that are used are without any consent, and the publication of the trademark is without permission or backing by the trademark owner. All trademarks and brands within this book are for clarifying purposes only and are owned by the owners themselves, not affiliated with this document.

Table of Contents

INTRODUCTION — 5

CHAPTER 1. HISTORY OF MACRAMÉ — 7

CHAPTER 2. KNOTS AND TECHNIQUES — 12
Lark's Head Knot — 13
Reverse Lark's Head Knot — 15
Capuchin Knot — 17
Crown Knot — 19
Diagonal Double Half-Knot — 21
Frivolité Knot — 23
Horizontal Double Half-Knot — 25
Josephine Knot — 26
Chinese Crown Knot — 28
Square Knot — 29
Half-knots and Square Knots — 30
Spiral Stitch — 32
Clove Hitch — 33
Overhand Knot — 34
Gathering Knot — 34

CHAPTER 3. TOOLS AND MATERIALS — 36
Yarn — 37
Hooks — 39
Wire — 40
Needles — 40
Tape — 41
Clothes Rack — 42
Cord — 42

CHAPTER 4. TIPS FOR NEAT KNOTTING — 48
Neatening the Rough Ends — 49
Cord Ends and Cord Caps — 51
Tying Knots — 55
Cord Fastenings — 56

CHAPTER 5. MACRAMÉ TROUBLESHOOTING — 58
Error 1 — 59
Error 2 — 59
Error 3 — 59
Error 4 — 59

CHAPTER 6. HOW TO DO A BUSINESS WITH MACRAMÉ — 61
How Can You Prevent Making Macramé Mistakes? — 62
Selling Macramé Items on Etsy Successfully — 62
Make a Connection with Your Buyers — 63
Stunning Photos — 64
Make Interesting and Accurate Item Descriptions — 64
Have Fast and Approachable Correspondence with Buyers — 64

CHAPTER 7. MACRAMÉ PLANT HANGERS AND HOME DÉCOR — 65
1. Modern Macramé Hanging Planter — 66
2. Mini Macramé Planters — 68

CHAPTER 8. CHRISTMAS PROJECTS — 69
3. Boho Christmas Tree — 70
4. Mini Macramé Christmas Ornaments — 71
5. 7-Point Snowflake — 74

CHAPTER 9. PERSONAL PROJECTS — 76
6. Heart Keychain — 77
7. Serenity Bracelet — 84
8. Lantern Bracelet — 87

CHAPTER 10. HOUSE PROJECTS — 90
9. Amazing Macramé Curtain — 91
10. Macramé Wall Art — 93
11. Hanging Macramé Vase — 96

CHAPTER 11. EASY MACRAMÉ PROJECT FOR BEGINNERS — 101
12. Mason Jar Wall Hanging — 102
13. Net Produce Bag DIY — 105
14. Macramé Placemats DIY — 107
15. Tassel and Macramé Key Chains — 109
16. Basic Tassel Keychain — 114

CHAPTER 12. ACCESSORIES — 118
17. Macramé Tie-Dye Necklace — 119
18. Macramé Watch Strand — 121
19. Macramé Gem Necklace — 122
20. Yarn Twisted Necklace — 124

CONCLUSION — 125

Introduction

Macramé is an intricate weaving technique with roots in South America and Africa. It looks difficult, but it actually requires little more than a couple of basic knots to get started.

This book will impart to you how to create several macramé projects. With these simple techniques under your belt, you'll be able to whip up something for yourself or your friends in no time at all.

If you are not familiar with the name macramé, the term is derived from the French word "macarrier," which means to tie together. This is how it got its name—tying together different strings of material was how the craft started centuries ago, just as weaving was an ancient method of making fabrics.

Macramé works well for a beginner because it requires only rope and knots.

This book will also provide the basic techniques for working with a macramé cord, step-by-step instructions for making the projects, and tips to help you get through all these difficulties.

You can make macramé in several ways—the two most common are knotting and weaving. The knots use one kind of cord while weaving uses braided or knotted material. Both methods of working involve knots, but bindings from tying off one piece of material to another as well as simple looping techniques are also used in both.

Anchoring pieces of materials to each other is very important in macramé. You cannot simply weave cord around items and hope for a good ending.

When making macramé, there are two kinds of knots you will encounter:

- Plain knots (butterfly knot, square knot, and arbor knot): These are your most basic knots. They look nice and they create fairly durable knots. If you're knotting something together by hand rather than using a Marcella cord/rope/string with no natural fiber content (fray-resistant), these should be your go-to type of knot. They are also good to use when making a series of knots in one string.
- Plaited knots: These knots look like braids and are particularly useful for heavy materials, such as leather or thicker rope. Plaited knots also hold up better to wear-and-tear (e.g., rubbing against clothes or furniture) because more strands of material are secured in the knot rather than two end pieces that can fray and break off over time with wear and tear.

Learn more as you progress through the stages of learning this craft and you will find that your experience with macramé rapidly improves, resulting in beautiful pieces you can be proud of.

Chapter 1

HISTORY OF MACRAMÉ

To offer people satisfaction in the things they need to use, that's one great design office; to give people enjoyment in the things they need to do, that's the other use of it. Although we may now consider the phrasing of this statement old-school, the heart of it still feels important. The theory of decoration by William Morris inspired a whole movement, and it still sounds true today. Think about it: the modern shopper wants to know more and more about story behind the producers and their products. The interest in Etsy shops and makers of small batches continues to increase, with many small brands now boasting cults.

The late 1800s arts and crafts movement focused on the value of crafts made with the hand, more specifically in reaction to rapid industrialization. Although it did not include just one style, it was made up of furniture, art, wallpaper, textiles, home decoration, and more. Focus: creating high-quality items that computers cannot do the same thing.

A knot is a simple action of connecting two loose ends together. We barely give a second thought to the action, but there's so much more to a knot. Since the earliest humans, Knots have been the constant companion of mankind, using them in practical application and transforming it into mystical, scientific, religious, medical, artistic, and decorative objects. Macramé is an example of how people turned the simple act of knotting into an art form.

The fragility of textile objects is a frustrating experience for archaeologists of problems—they disintegrate long before we can uncover them for analysis and documentation. This was the same problem with tracing the macramé's origins. Experts believe that knotting has been with mankind since the need for building and work was founded by man.

When so many people think about macramé, they imagine the fruits of the rising popularity of the textile technique in the 1970s—contraptions for hanging plants and glass tabletops, multi-tiered lamp shades, belts, bags, and other bohemian-favored accessories. While macramé fits in with other patterns from the period—the best way to set a boiling hot fondue pot on top of a macramé doily, obvs—its roots reach back thousands of years across oceans. Many believe that the term "macramé" is derived from the word "migramah," or "fringe" which is in Arabic. The first known "macraméers" were Arabic weavers from the 13th century, who began to secure the loose ends of woven textiles, such as towels and shawls by tying decorative knots.

Wherever and when macramé received its name, the technique is as old as its basic structure: the knot, which has an almost endless number of variations, countless practical applications, and caused an uncountable number of headaches when left to its own devices.

Excess folding and filling on sheets and veils are knotted in decorative fringes on the edge of hand-loomed fabrics by these craftsmen. The Spanish word macramé derives from the Arabic migramah, believed to mean "striped towel," "decorative fringe" or "embellished veil." After the Moorish conquest, the art was transported to Spain, then to Italy, particularly in the Ligurian region, and then spread across Europe. It was presented in England in the late 17th century at Mary II's court. Queen Mary taught her waiting ladies the art of macramé.

Macramé is mostly favored by women these days, like many fiber crafts, but some of the most famous and popular macromeres were men—sailors, to be more precise. Such sailors also started tying for months at sea and incorporating more practical uses, such as rope ladders and bell pulls. When the ships docked at different ports, the sailors often sold or bartered their jobs, and the macramé art—and the popularization of nautical products such as rope and twine —began to spread to other nations, including China, and what was then known as the "New World."

Sailors made macramé objects at sea in hours when they are not on duty, and when they landed, they sold or bartered them. British and American sailors of the nineteenth century made macramé hammocks, bell fringes, and belts. After most used frequent knots, they called the process "square knotting." Also called "McNamara's Lace" by sailors.

Sailors were not the only evangelists of the macramé. The Moors introduced Spain, which they occupied until the 15th century, to the Arabic knot-tying technique, and eventually, it moved to France and Italy. England Queen Marry II taught her ladies how to macramé in the 17th century; nearly 200 years, during Queen Victoria's reign and the subsequently dubbed Victorian Era, all fashion was the art form. Macramé details decorated everything from table linen to curtains to bedspreads and was a popular hobby for women of the period. A classic taught readers how to "work rich trimmings for black and colored costumes, for home wear, garden parties, seaside ramblings, and balls—fairy-like household and underlining decorations." Many Victorian homes were decorated with this craft.

The prominence of macramé faded in the early 1900s, the craft became much vaguer for more than half a century in both goods and practice. Yet people suddenly went back to madness for knots in the 1970s.

At the beginning of the feminist movement, Macramé's revival represented a broader cultural dichotomy—on the one hand, many of these women buckled traditional gender norms, such as marriage and motherhood, in search of empowered autonomy and financial and sexual freedoms; on the other, in their spare time, they resurrected an era known for its They w ere only wild, over-the-top, uninhibited, and grandiose in their approach to the painting. In the 1970s, you would imagine just about everything that was made of macramé.

Sure, the era's greatest macramé pattern was a complete hoot. The macramé owl's history, one of the most omnipresent and absurd examples of the craft, is somewhat enigmatic. Owls have been a popular theme in home decor in the 1970s, and the phenomenon may be related to the United States. The 1971 decision of the Forest Service to appoint Woodsy Owl as their mascot. Following President Richard Nixon's famous trip to China in 1972, Feng Shui became highly marketable in the U.S. and was the mature content for the growing New Age movement.

In 1977, the former home magazine of the Los Angeles Times not only marketed the macramé owl as the must-have home decor piece but also offered a $7.95 DIY kit. When in the early 1980s macramé went out of style again, thousands of once-treasured macramé owls were discarded. The survivors can still be seen in thrift shops and on Etsy and look just as dumb as the day they were born.

Macramé all but vanished during the 80s, 90s, and 2000s as a home decor trend, but the craft has made a steady return over the past five years. Modern bohemianism includes not only fashion and home decoration, but a whole lifestyle based on personal growth, spiritual development, and the importance of self-care, especially for women. Hobbies with a feminine heritage, including fiber arts such as macramé, have sparked interest; thanks to Facebook, eBay, Pinterest, and other social and e-commerce sites, modern macramé has sparked an interest.

We tried to hide things from the 70s very far away, as with many items from the 70s, and macramé vanished again. Popular artist medium. There have been dedicated artists since the 1970s who have brought macramé from a household craft to galleries of artists all over the world. And this is no different from our present day. Some people attend to the return of the macramé with the return of the houseplant phenomenon. This can also explain why ball plants have become a hit in Japanese art. But these are more expensive and difficult to manufacture and not suitable for all plants, so a plant hanger is a good alternative.

Macramé art was based on a number of practical artifacts. At the same time, artists in Portugal, Ecuador, and Mexico continued to develop chalks and purses as indigenous crafts, while macramé now focuses on several objects.

We now know that macramé took shape as a gateway to the world of mass production during the 60s and 70s as a portion of the massive revival in crafts. One idea that sounds real is the consciousness of the millennial generation of living a greener lifestyle and a desire to live closer to nature, but this is difficult for many in small apartments without a garden. So, it's the best thing to hang gardens. This may also be the reason why kokedamas Japanese art has become such a phenomenon.

Another interesting part is how macramé and other craft skills are used by different countries and their people as income in impoverished areas. Research suggests that macramé art has now been adopted in Ghana as one of the most important fashion accessory manufacturing methods. This art form is now an alternative method, particularly for the production of bags and shoes in the fashion industry. Over a few years, the number of younger consumers of macramé products has increased. Today's youth are trendy and focus on new creative designs. Today macramé art is not just a youth work, but a recognition of the creative development of Ghanaian youth's creativity.

Today, Macramé's talent and hobby mean many things to many people; in many respects, the talent is valuable and unique, although it doesn't matter to some. Macramé includes bonds that will secure the arms and hands. It can be very therapeutic and relaxing for the body, mind, and spirit to make a macramé product; it is also a choice for environmentally friendly art. These are just other of the benefits that macramé art lovers believe their practitioners derive from this art form.

Chapter 2

KNOTS AND TECHNIQUES

LARK'S HEAD KNOT

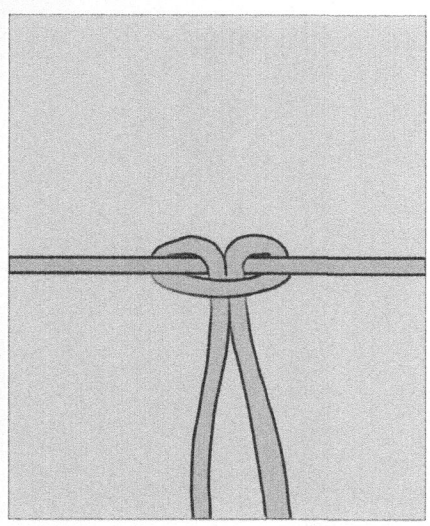

1. This is a boundless foundation knot for any venture and can be used as the foundation of the project. Use a lightweight cord for this; it can be purchased at craft stores or online, wherever you get your macramé supplies.

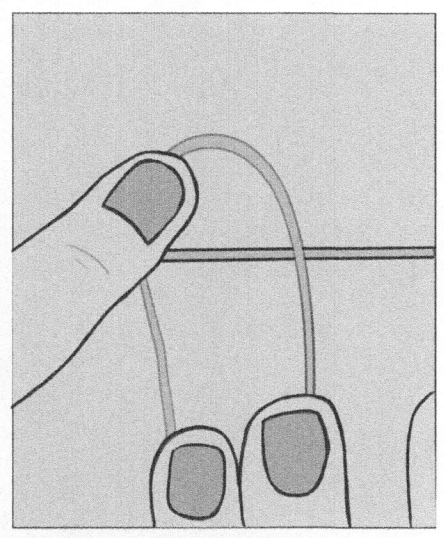

2. Watch the photos very carefully as you move along with this project and take your time to ensure you are with the correct string, at the correct point of the project.

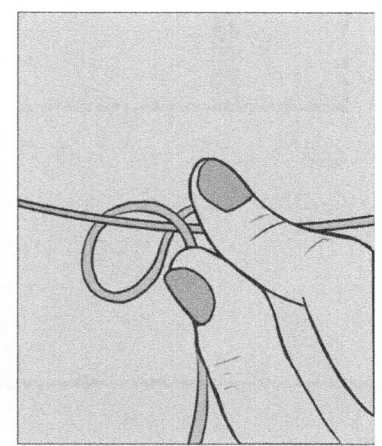

3. Use the base string as the core part of the knot, working around the end of the string with the cord. Make sure all is even, as you loop the string around the base of the cord.

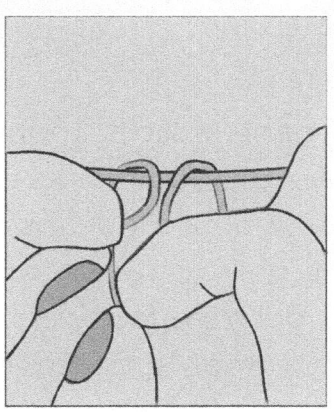

PAGE 13

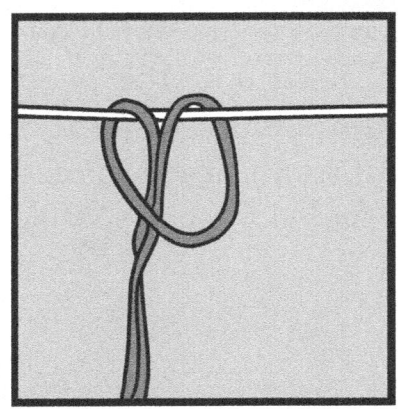

6. Make sure all is even and secure and tie off. Snip off all the loose ends, and you are ready to go!

4. Create a slip knot around the base of the string and keep both ends even as you pull the cord through the center of the piece.

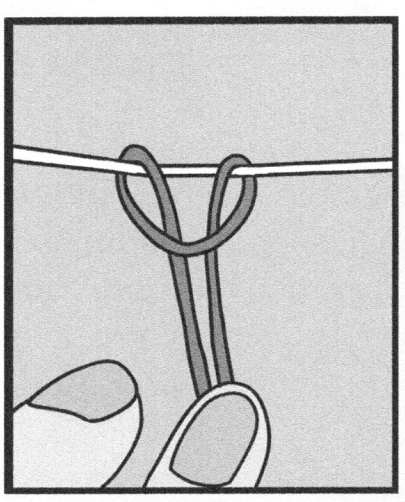

5. For the done project, make sure that you have all your knots secure and firm throughout and ensure it is all even. It is going to take practice before you can get it perfectly each time, but remember that practice does make perfect, and with time, you are going to get it, without too much trouble.

REVERSE LARK'S HEAD KNOT

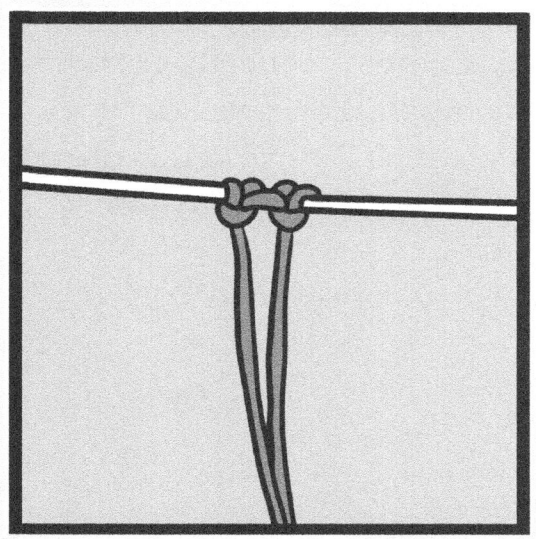

1. This is a great beginning knot and can be used as the foundation of the project. Use a lightweight cord for this; this again can be purchased at craft stores or online, wherever you get your macramé supplies.

2. Do not rush, and ensure you have even tension throughout. Practice makes perfect, but with the illustrations to help you, you will find it is not hard at all to create.

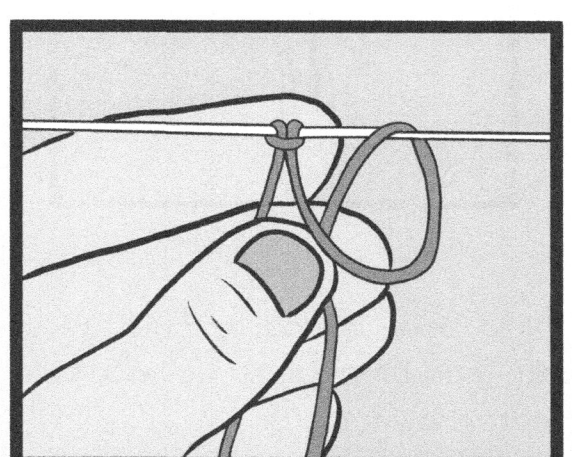

3. Use two hands to make sure that you have everything even and tight, as you work. You can use tweezers if it helps to make it tight against the base of the string.

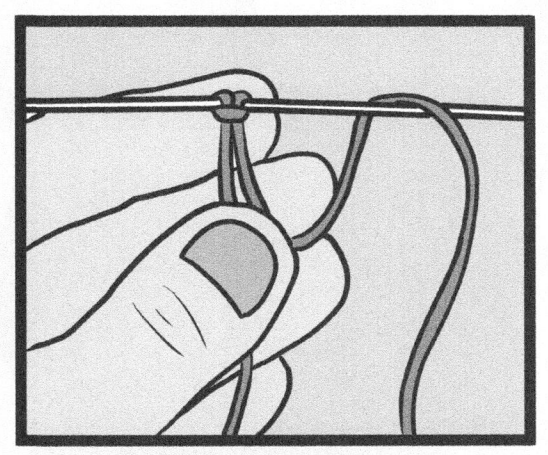

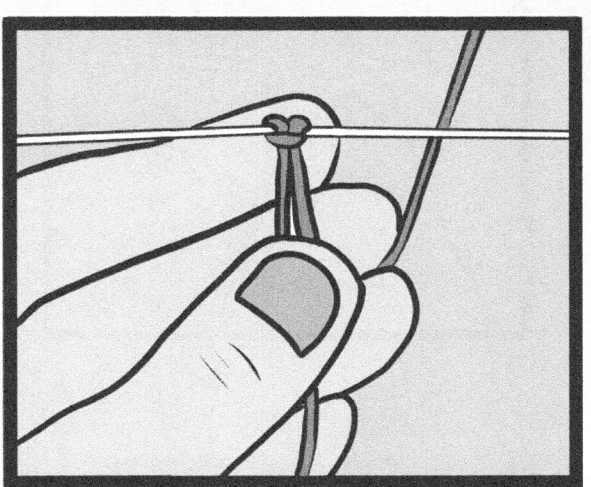

6. For the complete project, make sure that you have all your knots secure and firm throughout and ensure it is all even. It is going to take practice before you can get it perfectly each time, but remember that practice does make perfect, and with time, you are going to get it without too much trouble.

4. Utilize both hands to pull the string evenly down against the base string to create the knot.

5. Once more, keep the base even as you pull the center, creating a firm knot against your guide cord.

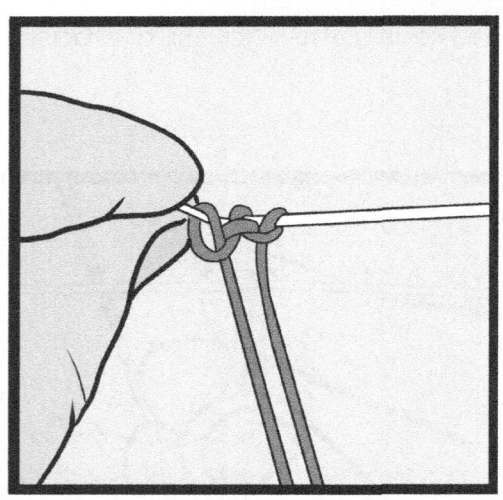

CAPUCHIN KNOT

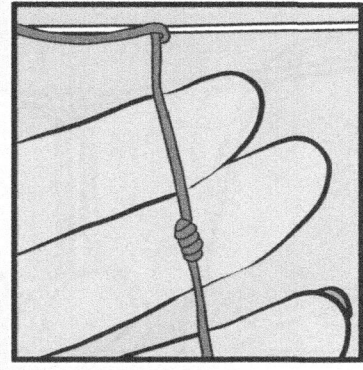

1. This knot for any project can be used as the foundation of the project. Use a lightweight cord for this.

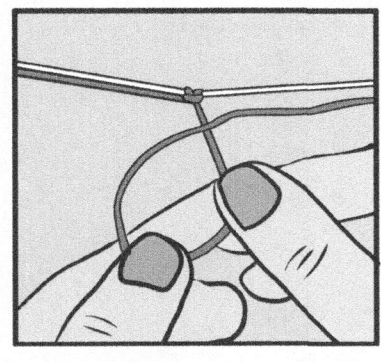

2. Watch the photos very carefully as you move along with this project and take your time to ensure you are using the correct string, at the right point of the project.

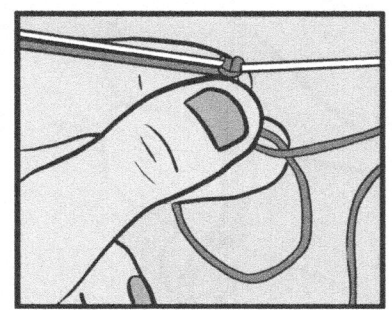

3. Start with the base cord, tying the knot onto this, and working your way along with the project.

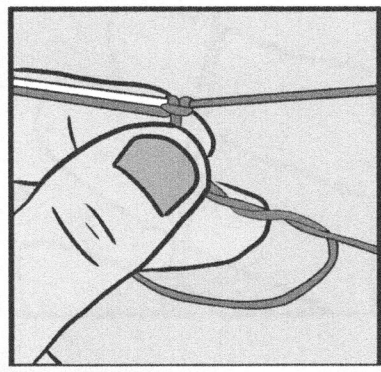

4. Twist the cord around itself two times, pulling the string through the center to form the knot.

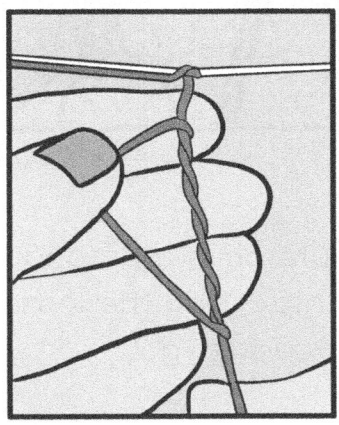

PAGE 17

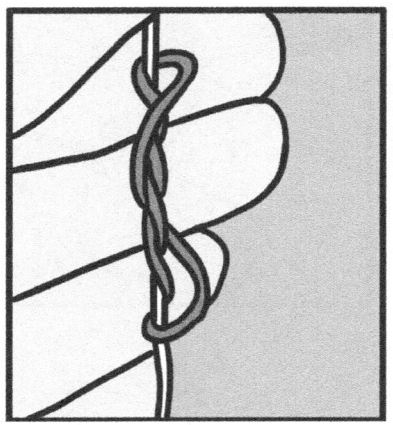

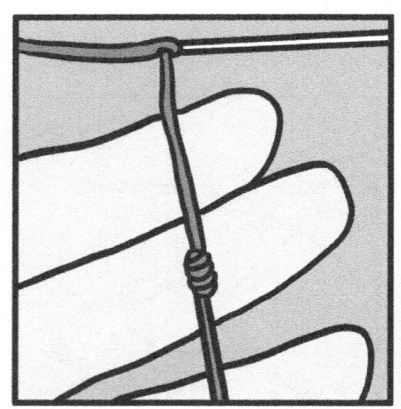
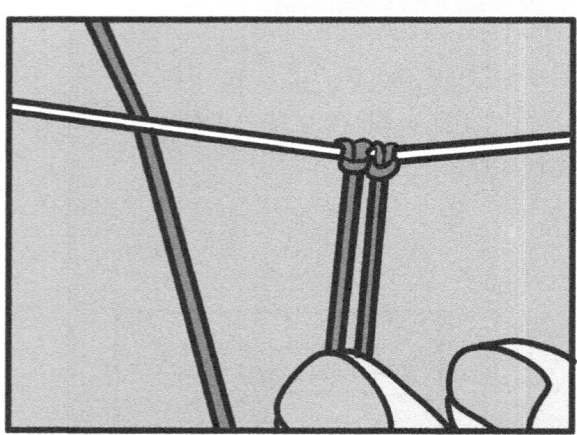

5. Make sure all is even and secure and tie off. Snip off all the loose ends, and you are ready to go!

CROWN KNOT

1. This is a great beginning knot and can be used as the foundation of the project. Use a lightweight cord for this.

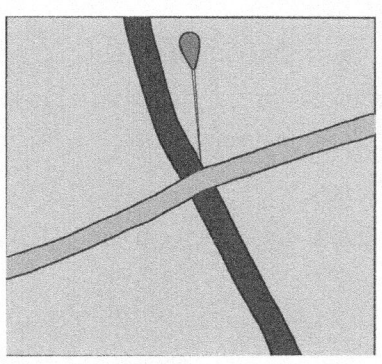

2. Never rush, then make sure you have even tension throughout. Practice makes perfect, but with the illustrations to help you, you will find it is not hard at all to create.

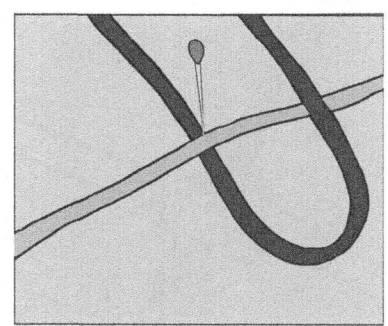

3. Use a pin to help keep everything in place as you are working.

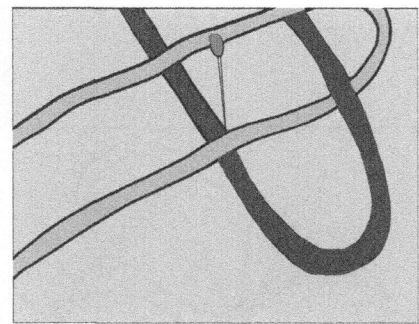

4. Weave the strings in and out of each other as you can see in the photos. It helps to practice with different colors, to help you see what is going on.

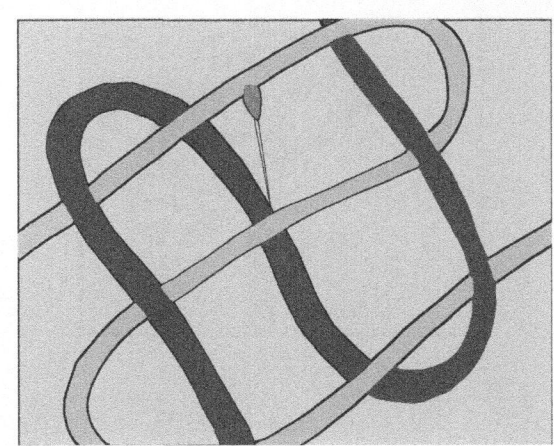

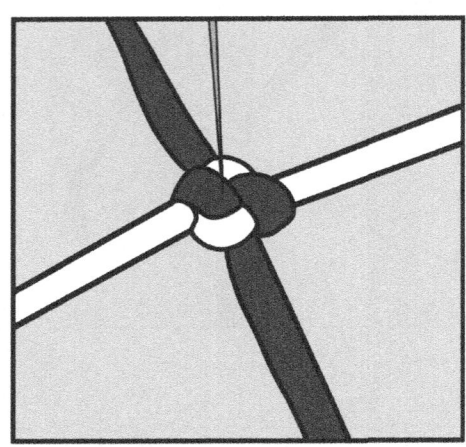

6. Stay to do this as often as you like to create the knot. You can make it as thick as you like, depending on the project. You can also create more than one length on the same cord.

5. Pull the knot tight, then repeat for the next row on the outside.

7. For the finished plan, make sure that you have all your knots secure and firm throughout and do your best to make sure it is all even. Make sure all is even and secure and tie off. Snip off all the loose ends, and you are ready to go!

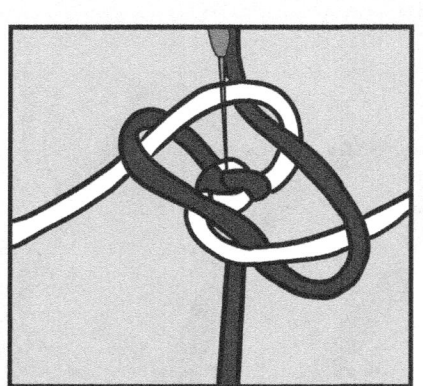

DIAGONAL DOUBLE HALF-KNOT

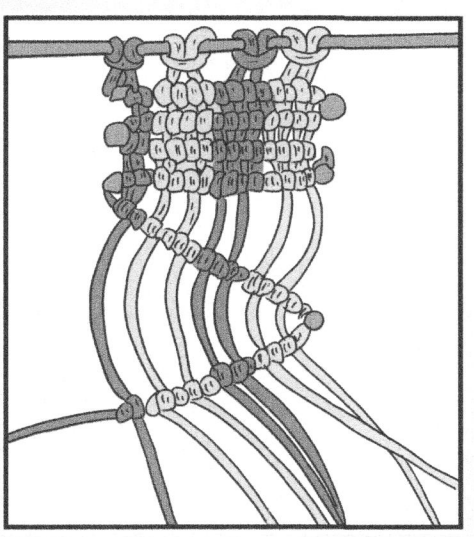

2. Do not rush, also make sure you have even tension throughout. Practice makes perfect, but with the illustrations to help you, you will find it is not hard at all to create.

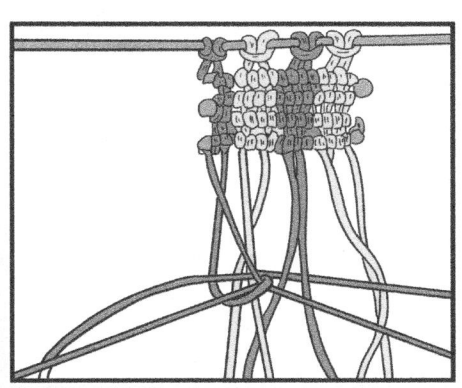

1. This is the seamless knot to use for decorations, basket hangings, or any projects that are going to require you to put weight on the project. Use a heavier-weight cord for this, which you can find at craft stores or online.

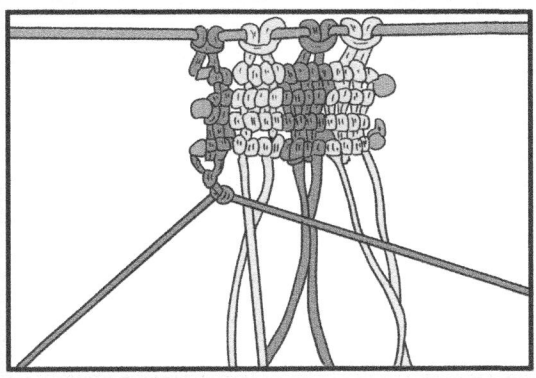

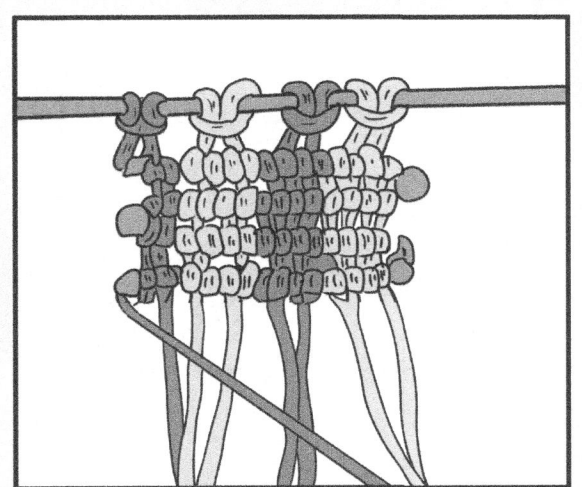

3. Twitch at the uppermost of the project then work your way toward the bottom. Keep it even as you work your way throughout the piece. Tie the knots at 4 inches intervals, working your way down the entire thing.

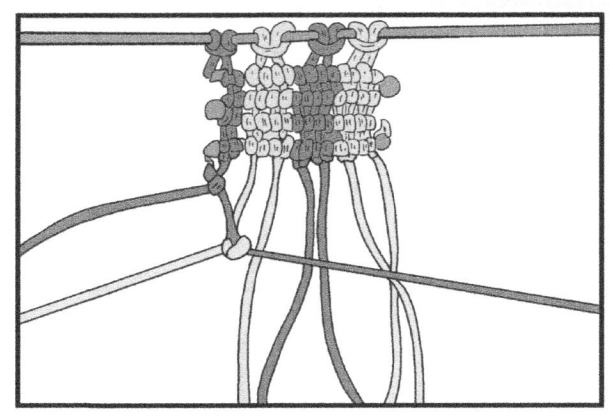

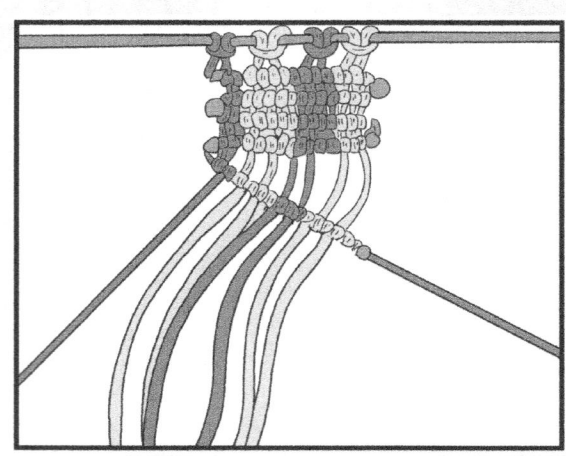

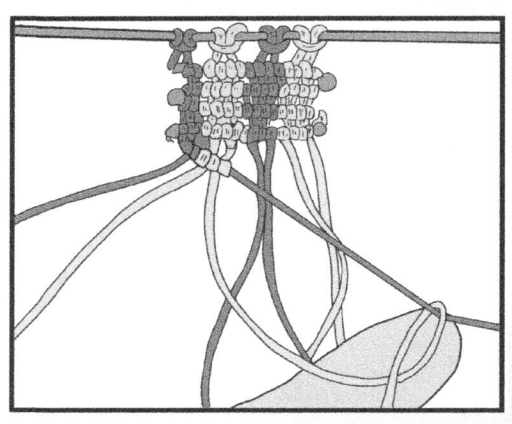

5. For the finished venture, make sure that you have all your knots secure and firm throughout, and do your best to make sure it is all even. Remember that practice does make perfect. Make sure all is even and secure and tie off. Snip off all the loose ends.

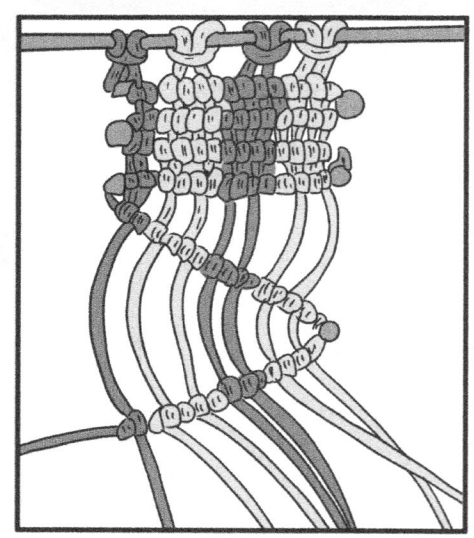

4. Weave in and out throughout, watching the photo as you can see for the right placement of the knots. Again, it helps to practice with different colors, so you can see what you need to do throughout the piece.

FRIVOLITÉ KNOT

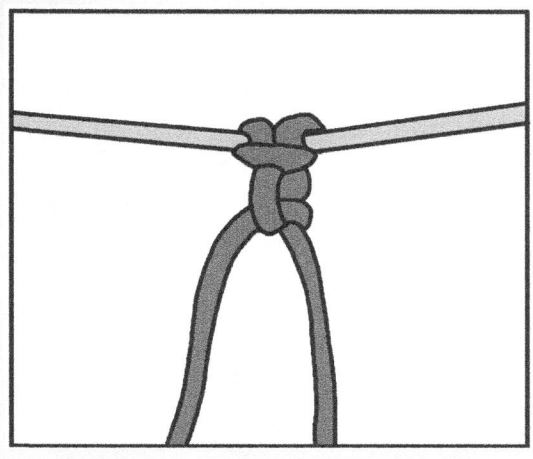

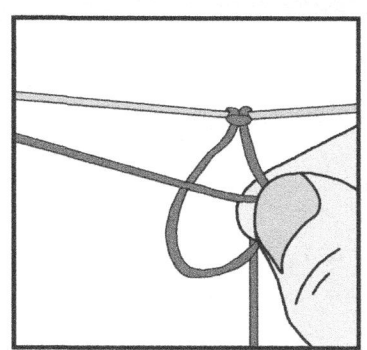

1. This can be used as the foundation for the base of the project. Use a lightweight cord for this too. It can be bought at craft stores or online.

3. Use the base string as the guide to hold it in place, then tie the knot onto this. This is a very straightforward knot; look at the photo and follow the directions you see.

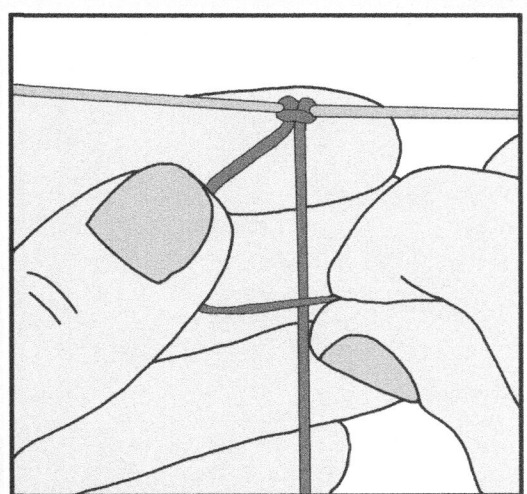

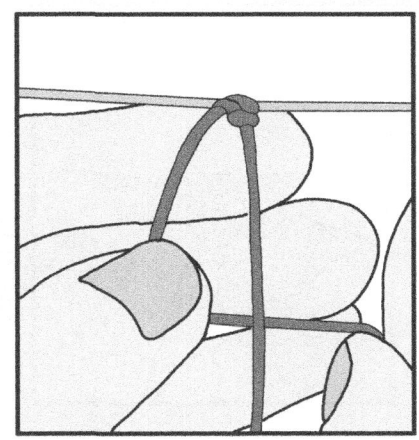

2. No need to rush, and make sure you have even tension throughout. With the illustrations to help you, you may find it is not hard at all to create.

PAGE 23

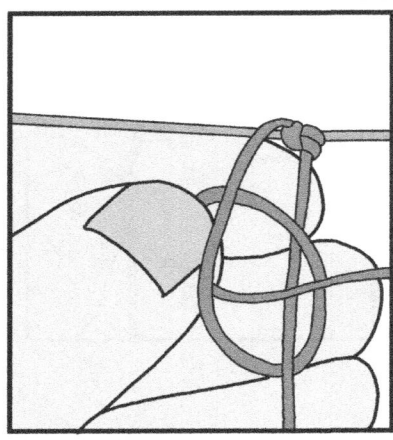

4. Pull the end of the cord, up and through the center.

5. When done, make sure that you have all your knots secure and firm throughout, and ensure it is all even. Make sure all is even and secure and tie off. Snip off all the loose ends.

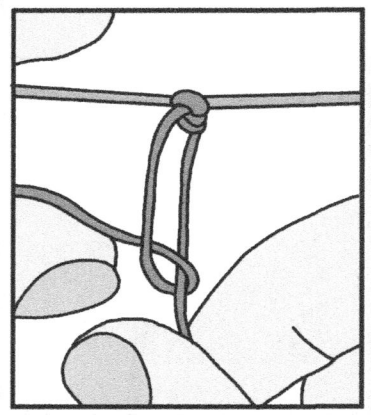

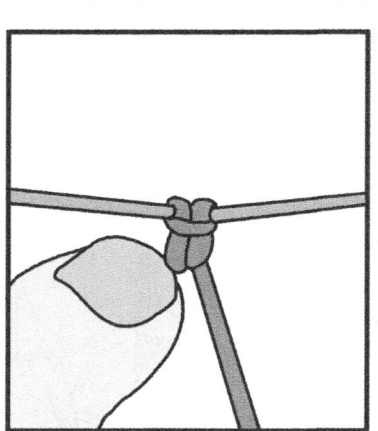

HORIZONTAL DOUBLE HALF-KNOT

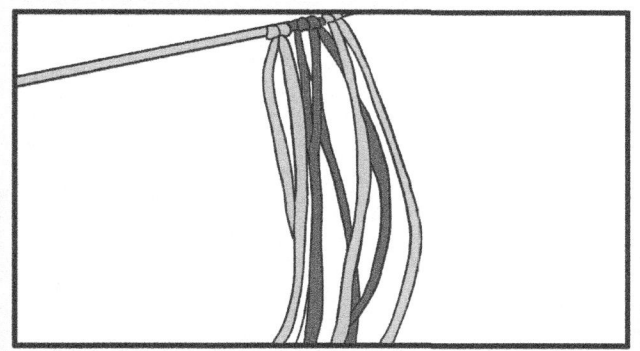

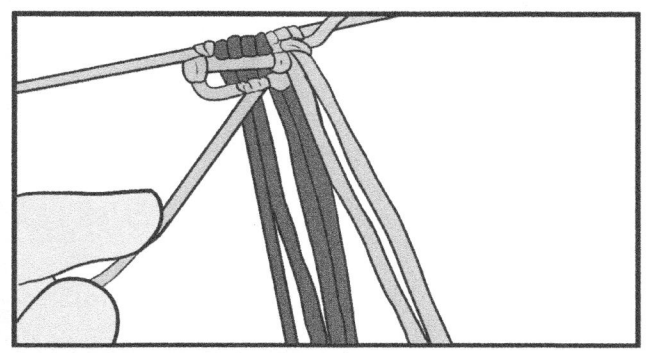

1. It can be used as the foundation for the base of the project. Use a lightweight cord for this by purchasing from wherever you get your macramé supplies.

perfect, but with the illustrations to help you, you will find it is not hard at all to create.

3. Twitch at the uppermost of the project then work your way toward the bottom. Keep it even as you work your way throughout the piece. Tie the knots at 4 inches intervals, working your way down the entire item.

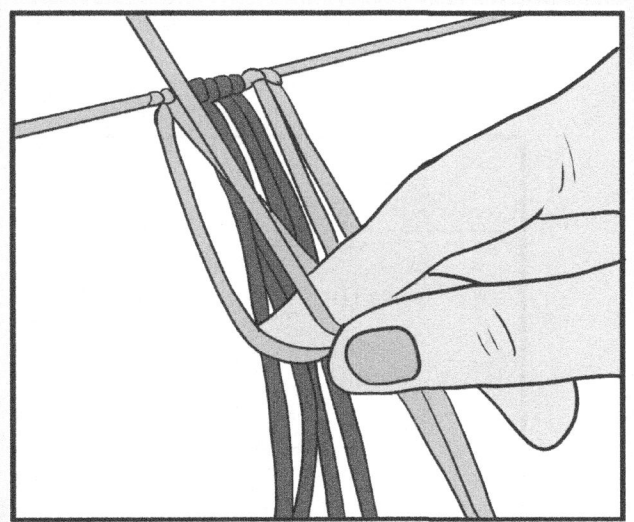

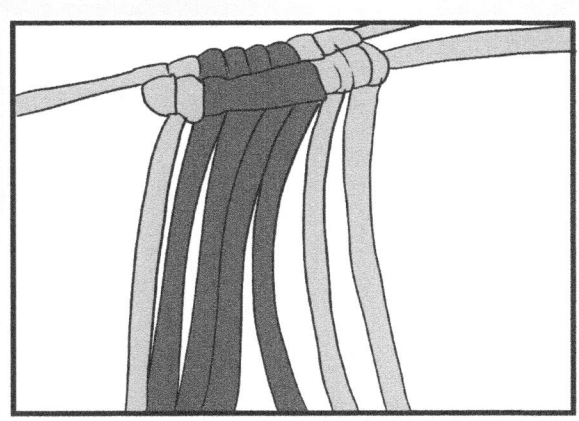

2. Follow the photos very carefully and take your time to make sure you are using the correct string at each point of the project. Make sure you have even tension throughout. Practice makes

4. Once finished, make sure that you have all your knots secure and firm throughout, and do your best to make sure it is all even. Make sure all is even and secure, and tie and snip off all the loose ends.

PAGE 25

JOSEPHINE KNOT

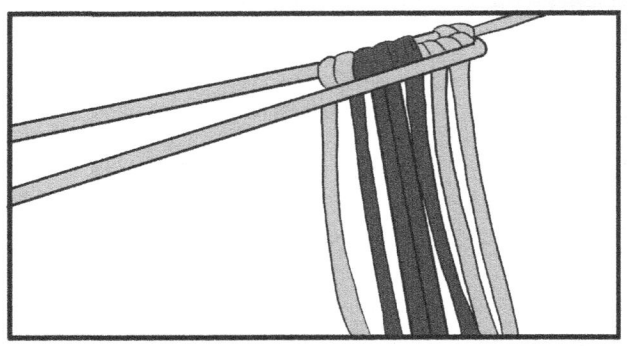

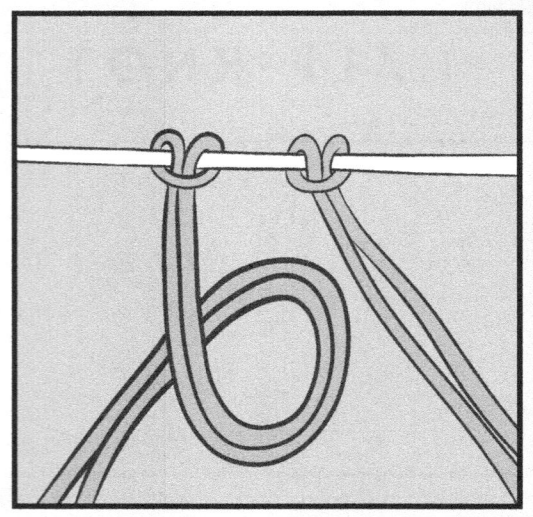

1. This is the ideal knot to use for decorations, basket hangings, or any projects that are going to require you to put weight on the project. Use a heavier-weight cord for this, which you can find at craft stores or online.

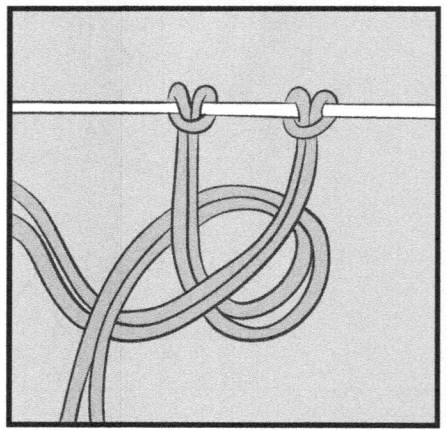

2. Follow the photos very carefully as you move along with this project. Take your time to correctly move the cords. Do not rush, and make sure the cords have even tension throughout.

5. If you are done, make sure that your knots are secure and firm, making sure they are all even. It is going to take practice before you can get it perfectly.

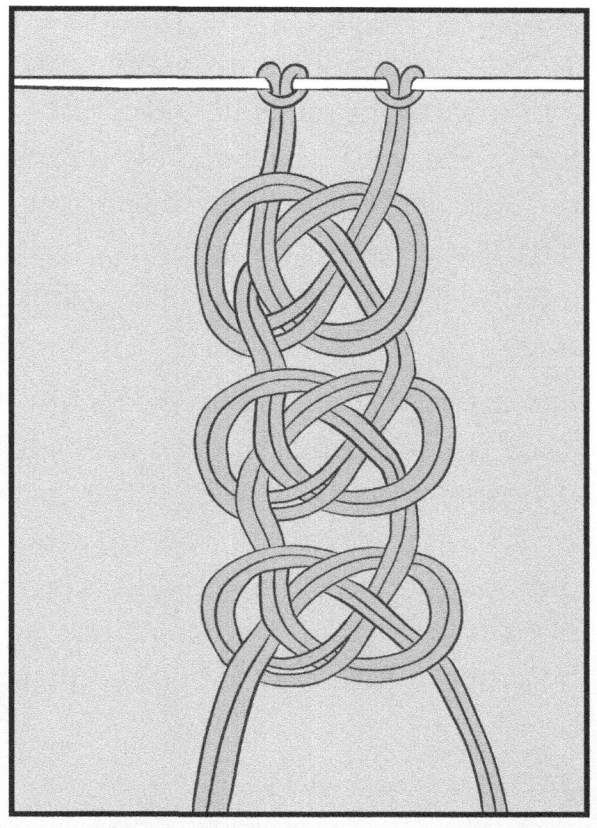

3. Use the pins along with the knots that you are tying, and work with larger areas simultaneously. This is going to help you keep the project in place, as you continue to work throughout the piece.

4. Pull the ends of the knots through the loops and form the ring at the center of the strings.

6. Make sure all is even and secure and tie off. Snip off all the loose ends.

PAGE 27

CHINESE CROWN KNOT

1. This can be used as the foundation for the base of the project. Use a lightweight cord for this—it can be purchased at craft stores or online, wherever you get your macramé supplies. Do not rush and make sure you have even tension throughout. Practice makes perfect but with the illustrations to help you, you will find it is not hard at all to create.

2. Use a pin to help keep everything in place as you are working. Weave the strings in and out of each other as you can see in the photos. It helps to practice with different colors to help you see what is going on. Pull the knot tight, then repeat for the row on the outside.

3. Continue to do this as often as you like to create the knot. You can make it as thick as you like, depending on the project. You can also create more than one length on the same cord.

4. For the finished project, ensure that you have all your knots secure and firm throughout and do your best to ensure it is all even. It is going to take practice before you can get it perfectly each time but remember that practice does make perfect and with time, you are going to get it without too much trouble.

5. Make sure all is even, secure, and tie off. Snip off all the loose ends and you are ready to go!

SQUARE KNOT

1. This is a great beginning knot for any project and can be used as the foundation for the base of the project. Use a lightweight cord for this—it can be purchased at craft stores or online, wherever you get your macramé supplies.

2. Do not rush and make sure you have even tension throughout. Practice makes perfect but with the illustrations to help you, it is not hard at all to create.

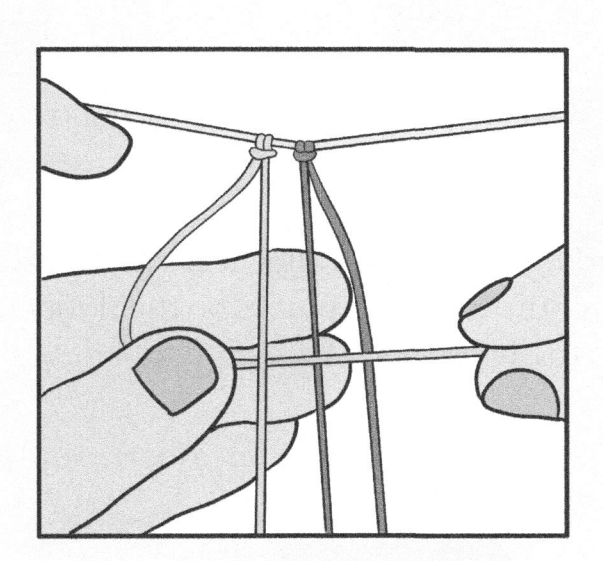

3. If you are finished, make sure that you have all your knots secure and firm throughout, and do your best to make sure it is all even. It is going to take practice before you can get it perfectly each time but remember that practice does make perfect and with time, you are going to get it without too much trouble.

4. Make sure all is even, secure, and tie off. Snip off all the loose ends and you are ready to go!

HALF-KNOTS AND SQUARE KNOTS

One of the most commonly used macramé knots is a square knot and it can also be generated as a left or a right-facing knot. The half-knot is actually half a knot in a rectangle. This may be left or right-facing, it entirely depends on which side you work from.

Square knots require at least four cords (two active cords and two filler strings) but may provide more. The Operating Strings are the first and final strings. We'll name them cord 1 and cord four running. The cables in the center are filler cables so we're going to list those two and three. Such cords swap locations but still maintain their initial numbering.

A square knot (left facing) on the left side of the completed knot has a vertical hump.

1. Take your first cord (operational cord 1) and pass it over the middle cords (filler cords two and three) to the right and under your final cord (operational cord 4.).

2. Take operational cord four and shift it under all filler cords and over operational cord one to the west.

3. Push all operating cords to close, leaving cords parallel to the filler. It is a half- square knot faced to the west. Functional cords currently swapped places on the right with functional cord 1 and operating cord four on the left.

4. Take running cord 1 and pass it over the two filler cords to the left and under operating cord four.

5. Take functioning cord four and shift it under all filler strings and overworking cord 1 to the right. Pull and tie all active strings.

6. Hold cables straight on the material. It completes the square knot to the left side.

A half-knot and square knot facing the right side of the completed knot has a vertical hump.

1. Remove the last cord (cord four) and transfer it over the filler cords (strings two and three) and under the first cord (cord 1) to the west.

2. Take working cord 1 and push it under the filler cords and over working cord four to the center.

3. Pull and lock all strings, making them clear. That is a half-square knot facing right.

4. Functional cords now have positions swapped and working cord one is on the right and working cord four on the left.

5. Take work cord four over to the side, over the cords of the filler, and underworking cord 1.

6. Take job cord 1 and shift it to the west, beneath the filler cords and above working cord four.

7. Pull and tie all active strings. It is a knot in a square facing right.

SPIRAL STITCH

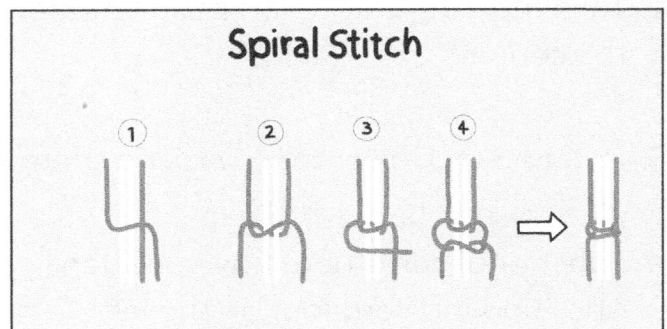

The spiral stitch, also known as a half-knot spiral or a half-knot sinnet, is a set of half-knots for spiral stitch formation. It is a decorative stitch that will be of great importance to your group. The spiral stitch requires at least four strings, two functioning strings, and two filler cords, although it may have more. Such strings are internally labeled 1 to 4 and shift from left to right. Strings 1 and four are the active strings and the filler cords are cords two and three. Such instructions explain how to create a spiral stitch on the left side, but you could also begin on the right-hand side and use half-knots on the correct side.

1. Take job cord 1 and push it over your filler cords to the right just under operating cord four.

2. Push working cord four to the west, and move under the cords of the filler but over your working cord one.

3. Remove all operating cords and stretch the cords around the filler.

4. Hold in the same direction as before, allowing further half-ties.

5. The cords will continue spiraling as you operate.

CLOVE HITCH

The Clove Hitch

In your ventures, the clove hitch, sometimes known as a double half hitch, generates a row. We may be employed vertically, horizontally, or diagonally on occasion.

A horizontal clove hitch is a series of knots that run through your macramé project. The first chord in the knot is your filler rope and the remainder of your cords are functioning cables.

1. Take the left cord and place your filler cable horizontally over the other strands.

2. To create a counter-clockwise circle, take your next cord (the first functioning cord) and carry it forward and then up and across the filler cord towards your left.

3. Take your same cord and take it up, though and across the circle, to the right of your first knot. Two ties will now lie next to each other. That is a hook tie parallel to the clove.

4. Undo the knots of the clove hook using your next operating rope along the same filler string.

5. Continue to build the ties before you have the knot or pattern that you seek.

For your project, a diagonal clove hitch produces a set of diagonal ties.

1. Take the chord at the left and place the filler chord diagonally between the other strings.

2. Follow measures two through four of the horizontal clove hitches, going diagonally rather than straight through.

3. Repeat before you have your perfect feel.

PAGE 33

OVERHAND KNOT

An overhand knot is a simple knot that ties together multiple cords. Different cables may be used or even one cable.

1. Stretch the string around a circle.

2. Move the ends of your strings to close around the coil.

GATHERING KNOT

Also known as a wrapping knot, the gathering knot is a closure knot that binds cords together. You can also find these at the end of the plant hangers for macramé. This knot comprises two functioning strings; the remaining strings are going to work as filler cords. You need to take a different cord length (it is going to be your working cord) and build a lengthy loop (u-shaped) above the filler cord ring, with the loop facing downwards.

1. Beginning below the functioning cord's top-end—which points upwards—wrap it across your filler cords and your string. Make sure you keep the loop exposed for a while.

2. Move the wrapping string end into the loop on the bottom of your wrappings.

3. Pick up one end of your cord—that's stuck out upwards—that will put the rope under your wraps.

4. Draw through the wraps before the coil

is enclosed. The knot inset is complete.

5. To get a smooth finish, cut both ends of your working cord if you wish.

The reverse lark head knot is performed in the opposite, so the hump is concealed in the back of your knot.

1. Split the rope in half and place the loop you just made under the dowel pin. Take the coil around the front side and drag the two cords the stretch around the thread.

2. This is a good beginning knot for any project and can be used as the foundation for the base of the project. Use a lightweight cord for this—it can be purchased at craft stores or online, wherever you get your macramé supplies.

3. You need not rush and make sure you have even tension throughout. Practice makes perfect but with the illustrations to help you, you will find it is not hard at all to create.

4. Use two hands to make sure that you have everything even and tight as you work. You can use tweezers if it helps to make it tight against the base of the string.

5. Use both hands to pull the string evenly down against the base string to create the knot.

6. Again, keep the base even as you pull the center, creating a firm knot against your guide cord.

7. For the finished project, make sure that you have all your knots secure and firm throughout and do your best to make sure it is all even. It is going to take practice before you can get it perfectly each time but remember that practice does make perfect and with time, you are going to get it without too much trouble.

8. Make sure all is even, secure, and tie off. Snip off all the loose ends and you are ready to go!

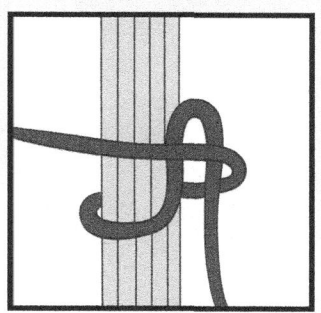

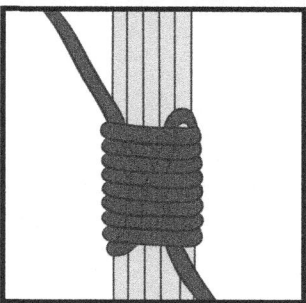

Chapter 3
TOOLS AND MATERIALS

YARN

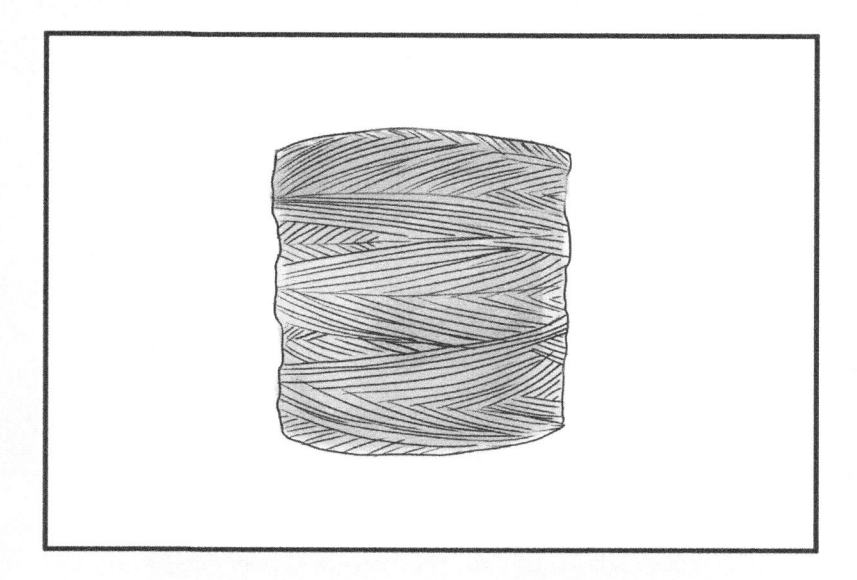

While you can use any yarn, as a beginner, you will find it best to use the yarn options we will outline below since they are easier to work with than others.

Choosing the Best Yarn for Macramé

- **Fiber type:** Choose from both plant and animal fibers.

- **Acrylic yarn:** Acrylic is generally a popular yarn among crochet enthusiasts. It is usually among the affordable choices for yarn, comes in a variety of colors, and is widely available. It is a more-than-acceptable choice for you as a beginner.

- **Cotton yarn:** It's an inelastic fiber, thereby making it a bit more challenging to work with than wool. However, where you want the item to hold its shape, this quality makes cotton an excellent choice for specific projects.

- **Wool yarn:** Wool is the perfect choice for you to practice your stitches. It is forgiving of mistakes and is a resilient fiber. If you happen to make a mistake while crocheting, most wool yarns are natural to unravel and even re-use (in crochet, it's called frogging). Wool yarn is not suitable for those with wool allergies, but for most, it is the right crocheting choice.

Additional Yarn Tips and Considerations

- **Yarn weight:** Yarns come in different thicknesses as well. This thickness is what we refer to as weight. The importance of the yarn is usually found on the label, where it's numbered 1 to 7 (from the thinnest to the thickest). It is most comfortable to work with a worsted weight yarn as a beginner, which is #4 on the yarn label.

Note: You should use the correct crochet hook size for the yarn weight you will be using.

- **Yarn color:** Choose lighter yarn colors rather than dark ones, as it can get challenging to see your stitches if using yarns with dark ones.

- **Yarn texture:** Choose smooth yarn and not textured ones. As you begin crocheting, avoid eyelash yarns and any other textured novelty yarns, which can get quite frustrating to work with.

- **Yarn yardage:** Each ball of yarn has different yardage amounts, which relates to the price. You can find two balls of yarn at the same rate; check the yardage to ensure the value of yarn in each ball is approximately the same.

- **Yarn price:** The price of yarn varies significantly from brand to brand and fiber to fiber. It is better to work on the affordable ones so that you get the hang of them before investing a lot of money in very expensive yarns. Therefore acrylic, wool, and cotton are the top fiber choices, as they tend to be the most affordable.

- **Yarn color dye lot:** to crochet will need more than one ball of yarn; then, you want to ensure that all the colors match (assuming that you are using the same colorway or color for the entire project). You do this by checking the "dye lot on the yarn label to ensure that the balls have noticeable differences between them.

- **Washing details:** This will be important if you are crocheting something to wear. For instance, you can use wool that is safe to put in the washer and dryer, or you can do so for some wool that must be hand-washed and dried flat because it will sink in the dryer. The yarn label contains this information to aid in your selections.

HOOKS

The average crochet hook works for anyone, and it favors beginners like you. You will find crochet hooks sold at yarn stores or any major craft retailer. You can also get them online. Few things you need to know about:

- **Material**: A basic crochet hook can be made of several common elements such as bamboo, plastic, and aluminum. Most people usually choose aluminum crochet hooks for their first project. There are also fancier crochet hooks made of wood, glass, and clay.

- **Size:** Crochet hooks differ in size; many different formats are measured in numbers, letters, or millimeters. For instance, a basic crochet hook set may range from E–J. A general-sized crochet hook is normally H-85 mm. Size E is smaller than size H; size J is more significant. As mentioned, you should match the size of your crochet hook with the weight of your yarn, which is usually on the label of the yarn. For most beginners, it is generally advisable to work with a size G or H crochet hook and worsted- weight yarn.

- **Hook throat:** an inline or tapered less or more flatness to the head of the hook. Since neither is better than the other, if you find it hard to work with one, try the other.

WIRE

The wire is a hard material to use for macramé—but if you master the craft, the results can be unique pieces of jewelry. The essence of metal is not to bend repeatedly. It lacks strength, and repetitive bending causes the wire to become brittle and work-hardened. If you bend it back and forth, again and again, it will finally crack. Heavier wire also doesn't like to bend without a huge amount of effort. Most metal macramé is made from thinner gauge wire, which is easier to manipulate. When it's working, it will always stiffen, but the less you bend it, the better.

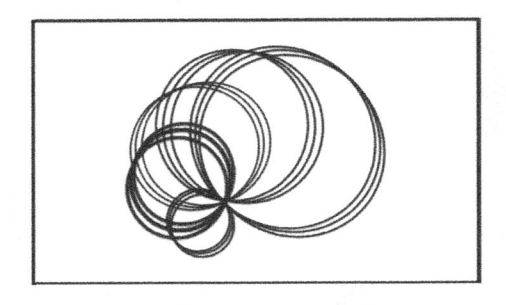

NEEDLES

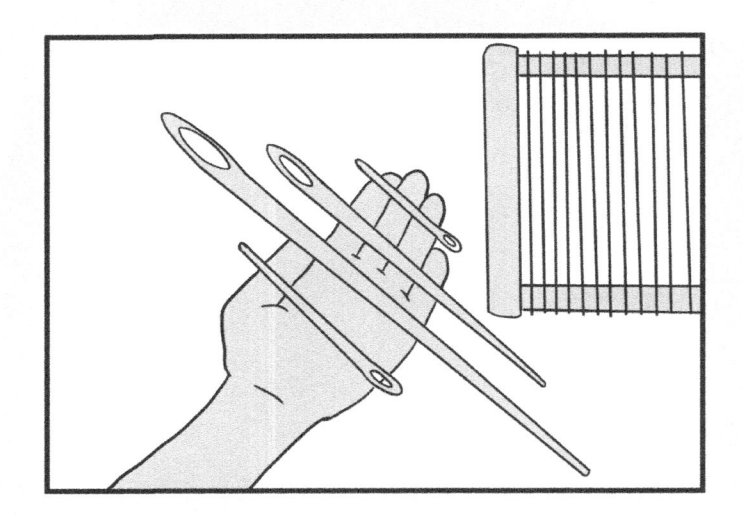

Various materials have various grindings and unexpectedly grasp the yarn; smooth needles, such as metallic needles, help quick knitting, while more unpleasant needles, such as bamboo, offer more erosion and are this way less inclined to dropping join. The knitting of new lines happens just at the decreased finishes. Needles with lit tips have been offered to permit knitters to weave in obscurity.

TAPE

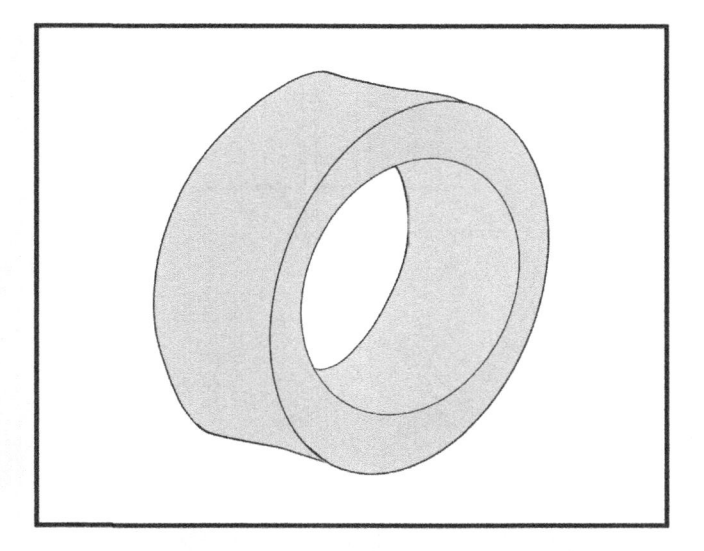

Use tape on the ends of your cords to keep them from fraying. I suggest masking tape since it will not leave any marks on the cord. When cutting a cord, you can first put tape on the part where you will reduce the cord. Cut in the exact half of the tape to have the end and the beginning of the next cord with tape. Use tape on the terms of your cords to keep them from fraying. I suggest masking tape since it will not leave any marks on the cord. When cutting a cord, you can first put tape on the part where you will reduce the cord. Cut in the exact half of the tape to have the end and the beginning of the next cord with tape.

CLOTHES RACK

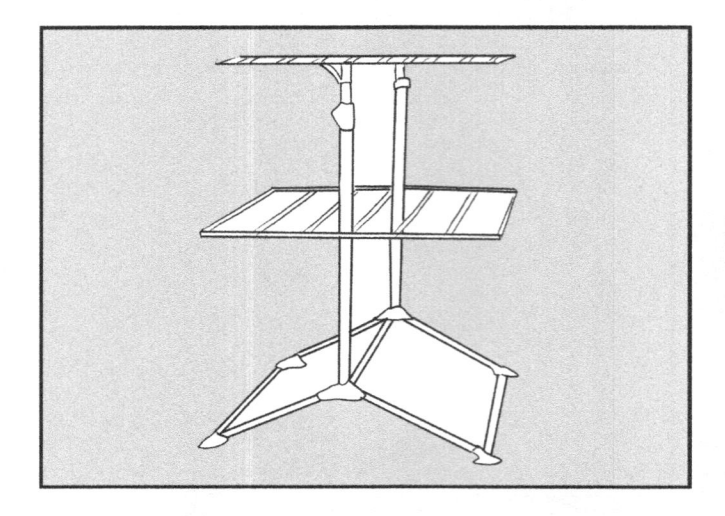

To work comfortably, it is recommended to use a clothes rack. Any type of clothes rack will do, although one that is adjustable in height can be helpful. Something like a clothes frame can also work: a curtain rail or wooden step ladder might work.

CORD

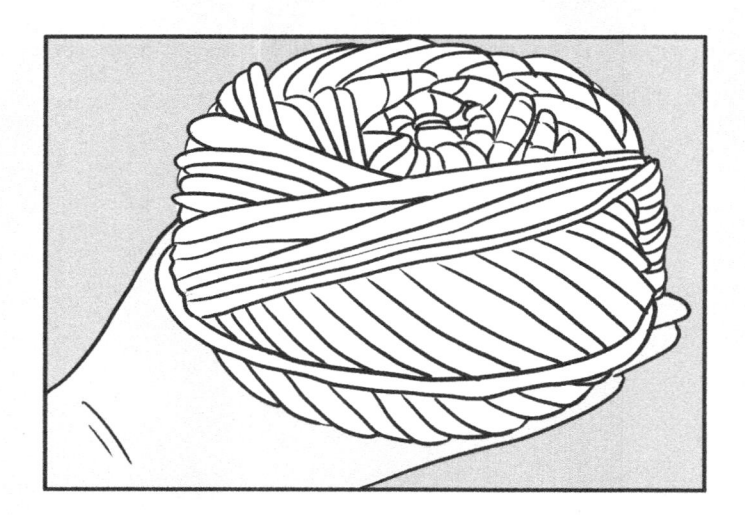

Cotton is very soft and pleasant to work with, while jute, for instance, could hurt your hands while working with it. T-shirt yarn is cheap and quite easy to find. But it would help if you considered that most of the T-shirt yarn tends to be a bit elastic, which makes it less suitable for hanging objects that must carry some weight like plant hangers.

Types of Cord

Macramé stylists make use of different types of materials. The materials can be classified in two major ways: natural materials and synthetic materials.

Natural Materials

The qualities of natural materials differ from synthetic materials and knowing these qualities would help you to make better use of them. Natural cord materials existing today include jute, hemp, leather, cotton, silk, and flax. There are also yarns made from natural fibers. Natural material fibers are made from plants and animals.

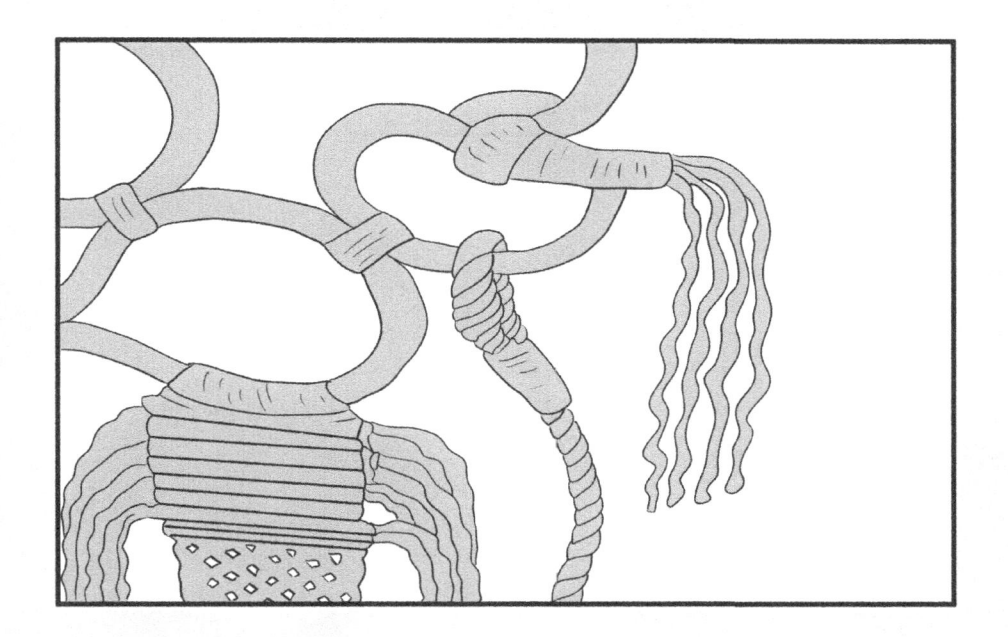

Synthetic Materials

As natural materials, synthetic materials are also used in macramé projects. The fibers of synthetic materials are made through chemical processes. The major ones are the nylon beading cord, olefin, satin cord, and parachute cord.

Cord Measurement

Before you can embark on a macramé project, it is essential that you determine the amount of chords you will need. This includes knowing the length of the required cord and the total number of materials you must purchase.

Equipment: To measure, you will need paper for writing, a pencil, a tape rule, and a calculator. You would also need some basic knowledge of unit conversion as shared below:

- 1 inch = 2.5.4 millimeters = 2.54 centimeters
- 1 foot =1.2 inches
- 1 yard = 3 feet = 3.6 inches
- 1 yard = 0.9 meters

Note: The circumference of a ring = 3.14 * diameter measured across the ring.

Measuring Width

The first thing to do is to determine the finished width of the widest area of your project. Once you have this width, pencil it down.

Next, determine the actual size of the materials, by measuring their width from edge to edge.

You can then proceed to determine the type of knot pattern you wish to use with the knowledge of the knot pattern. You must know the width and spacing (if required) of each knot. You should also determine if you want to add more cords to widen an area or if you would need extra cords for damps.

With the formula given above, calculate and determine the circumference of the ring of your designs.

Determine the mounting technique to be used. The cord can be mounted to a dowel, ring, or other cord. Folded cords affect both the length and width of the cord measurement.

Cord Preparation

Though usually rarely emphasized, preparation of the cords and getting them ready for use in macramé projects is one of the core pillars of the art of macramé. At times, specialized processes such as conditioning and stiffening of cords need to be carried out before macramé projects can be begun. In general, however, cord preparation in macramé is mainly concerned with dealing with cut ends and preventing these ends from unraveling during the project. During the course of a project, constant handing of materials can distort the ends, which can end up having disastrous consequences on your project. Before starting your project, if you do not appropriately prepare special kinds of cords, like ones that were made by the twisting of individual strands, that cord is likely to come apart, effectively destroying your project completely.

Therefore, cord preparation is extremely and incomparably important to the success of any macramé project, the preparation of each cord is meant to be done during the first step of making any knot, which is the step where you cut out your desired length of cord from the larger piece.

For cord conditioning, experts recommend rubbing beeswax along the length of the cord. To condition your cord, simply gets a bit of beeswax, let it warm up a bit in your hands, and rub it along the cord's length. This will help prevent unwanted tight curls on your cord. Note that beeswax may be applied to both natural and synthetic materials. For synthetic materials, however, only Satin and fine Nylon beading cords compulsorily require conditioning. After conditioning, inspect your cords for any imperfections and discard useless pieces to ensure the perfection of your project. After conditioning, then comes the actual process of cord preparation. Cords can be prepared (i.e., the ends can be prevented from fraying) using a flame, a knot, tape, and glue.

To prevent the unraveling of your cord using a flame, firstly test a small piece of the material with the flame from a small lighter. The material needs to melt, not burn. If it burns, then such a cord is not suitable for flame preparation. To prepare using a flame, simply hold the cord to the tip of the flame for 2 to 5 seconds, and make sure the cord does not ignite but melts. Flame preparation is suitable for cords made from olefin, polyester, and nylon, and the process is compulsory for the preparation of parachute cords.

Tying knots at the end of the cord is another effective method to prevent fraying. The overhand knot is an all-time favorite, but knots such as the figure 8 knot, which is best suited to flexible cords, can be used if you think the knot might have to be undone at some point in your project. The Stevedore knot can be used to prevent fraying when using slippery materials.

Glue is another priceless alternative that can be used to prevent fraying at the ends of cords efficiently. However, not all kinds of glue may be used in cord preparation. Only certain brands, such as the Alien's Stop Fray, may be used in cord preparation. Household glue might also be used, but only when diluted with water. To prepare your cord, simply rub the glue on the ends of the material and leave it to dry. If you intend to pass beads over the glued end, roll the cord's end between your fingers to make it narrower as it dries. Nail polish may also be used as an alternative to glue.

Simply wrap the tape around the end of the cord where you want to prevent fraying of your material. Make sure the end of the cord remains narrow by squeezing it between your fingers. It is advisable to use masking tape or cellophane tape for your preparations.

A special class of macramé cords, known as a parachute cord, requires a special form of preparation. To prepare a parachute cord, pull out the core yarns from the sleeve, and expose the yarns by about half an inch. Now cut the core yarns back, so that they become even with the outer sleeve, and then push the sleeve forward till the yarns become invisible. To complete the preparation, apply flame to the outer sleeve till it melts, and then press the handle of your lighter onto the sleeve while it's still warm to flatten the area and keep it closed up. The melted area will look darker and more plastic than the rest of the material.

Finishing Techniques

Finishing techniques refer to the methods by which the ends of cords after knots have been created may be taken care of to give a neat and tidy project. Finishing is often referred to as tying off. Several finishing knots are available and are extremely effective methods for executing finishing processes. Reliable finishing knots include the overhand knot and the barrel knot.

Folding techniques are also dependable finishing techniques. For flexible materials like cotton, all you need to do is fold the ends flat against the back surface and add glue to the ends to hold them in place. For less flexible materials, fold the cords to the back, then pass them under a loop from one or more knots, and then apply glue, allow it to dry, and cut off excess material.

Finally, you can do your finishing with the aid of fringes. You may choose between a brushed fringe and a beaded fringe.

Chapter 4

TIPS FOR NEAT KNOTTING

All knotting methodologies have at least a single raw edge to create a piece of jewelry, accessory, or another item that must be covered or neatened in some manner. Conventional methods like button knots or whipping use the knotting string itself to hide all the raw ends or you may use a wide variety of specially made tools and fastenings for this task.

NEATENING THE ROUGH ENDS

Cords and braids begin to protrude at the top edge, so the top must be neatened to some degree to incorporate it into a finding. You may use different methods to neaten rough edges, but which one you use depends on the number of strings and the form of material used.

Meltdown

While using a nylon knotting cord (KC) or the paracord, neaten the end by holding it in a flame for about a second or two-a domestic gas lighter is enough to burn up the side and fuse its raw ends.

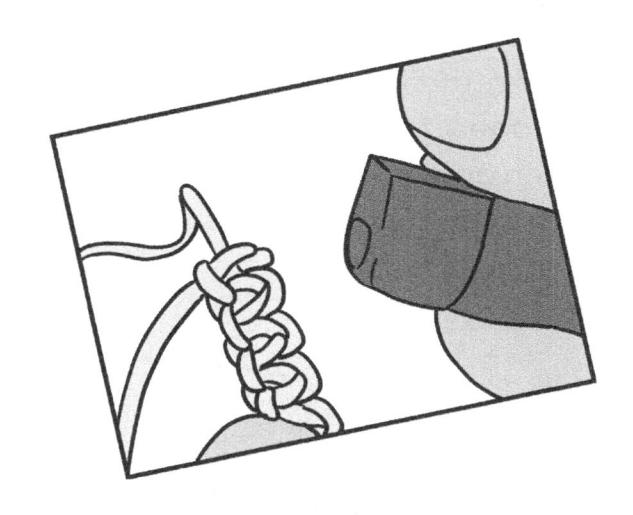

Tip: Always take good care not to burn your hands when melting the edges of your strings using a gas lighter.

Wrapping

Use a stable sewing or beading thread, or some fine wire to complete braids or string ends before adding a finding. This technique gives a little extra breadth to the string.

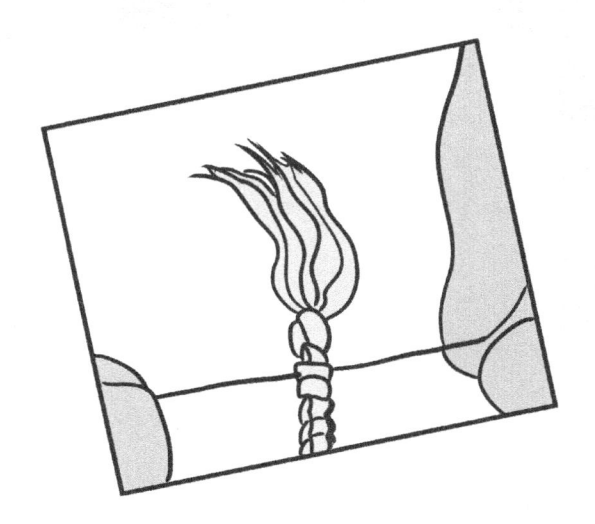

1. Working close to the end of the string ties the thread or wire tightly around the edge of the string so that the binding is even and the end of the cord is hidden underneath. Don't overwrap, or that's going to be too heavy.

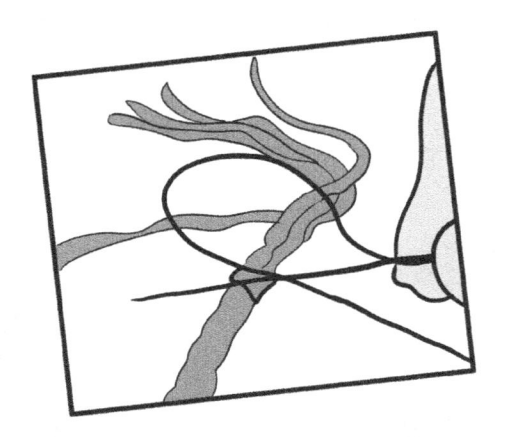

2. Using a sewing needle sew the tail underneath the wrapped strings (WC). Trim the access tail, if required, over the top of your cord as well.

Whipping

A thicker string should be used for a stylish whipped end (WE). This method can also be used for building a loop on a single end or around a double cord, as can be seen here.

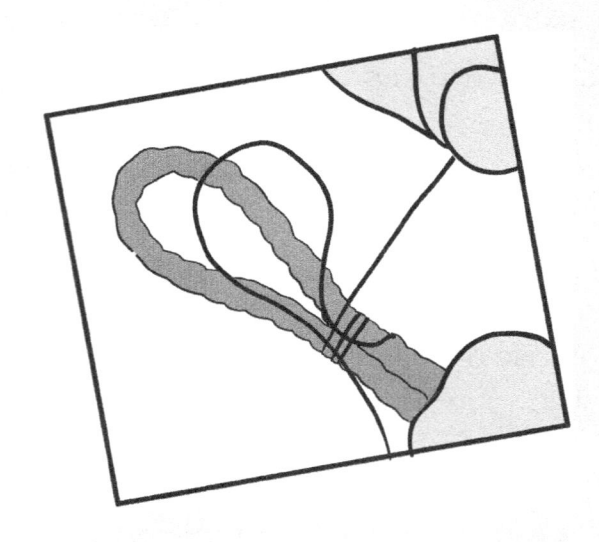

1. Start making a narrow string loop and put it on the top edge at the edge of your braid or looped braid. From the bottom edge, start coiling your working end (WE) around the braid and over both the loop cords (LC) several times.

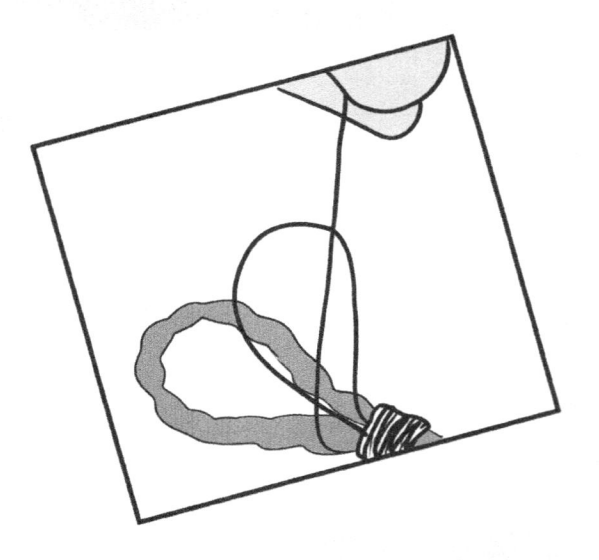

2. Keep on wrapping the fine string to form a single wrapping depth. Keeping the strings clean and tidy when wrapping, put the working end (WE) of the string into the circle formed.

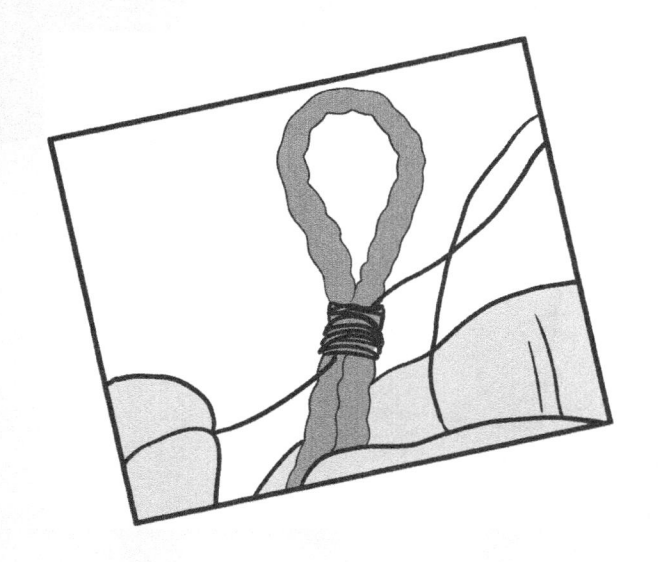

CORD ENDS AND CORD CAPS

Cord ends are tiny metal finds made to hide one or two raw edges. End caps that may be oval, rectangular or square, are wider than the ends of the cord and ideal for a wider rope or braid. All types include either a sturdy loop or an opening for the insertion of a fastening. The internal distance or length of the finding must be compared to the thickness or width of the cord or braid.

3. Try pulling the tail of the slender string's loop and then drag to hide the thread under the whipping. Trim all tails neatly.

4. Finishing with ends of the string, end caps, and cones.

There are several kinds of cord end, an end cap or cone is appropriate for completing the rough edges, and some of the wide variety is covered in.

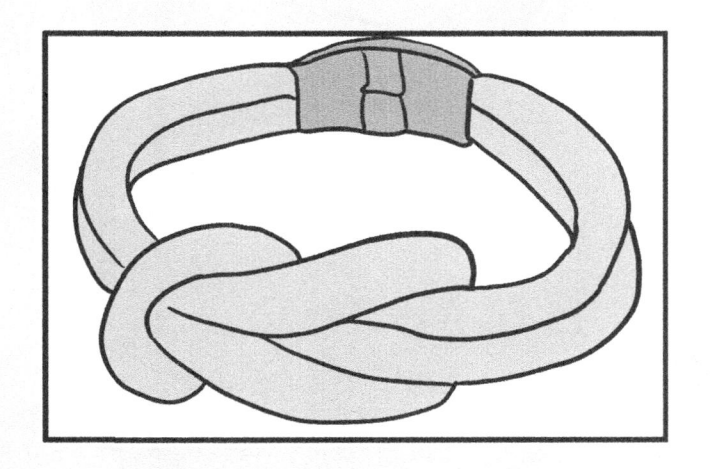

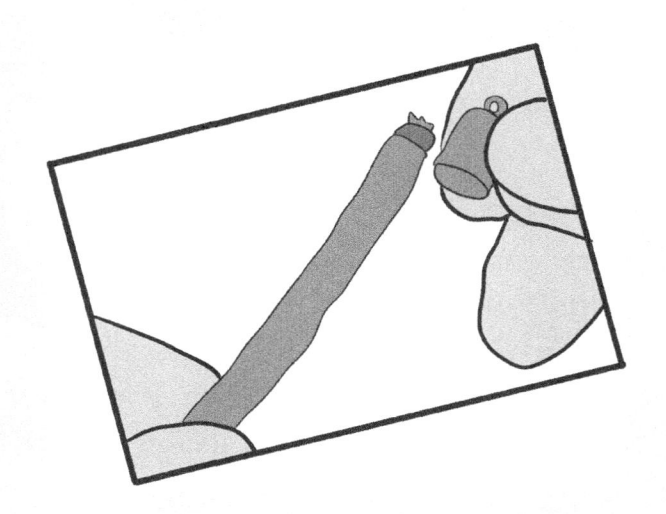

Fitting an End Cap or Cone

1. Tie the edge of the braid (or bundle of cords) with a thin stitching or beading string, make sure that the wrapping is not too thick to conceal inside the end cap; cut smoothly.

1. Tie or whip the ends of the bundle of strings or braid or some fine wire, make sure that the end cap will still fit over. Bend the headpin over maybe 6 mm. (¼in) from the end and push it under the 14 wrapping as displayed below.

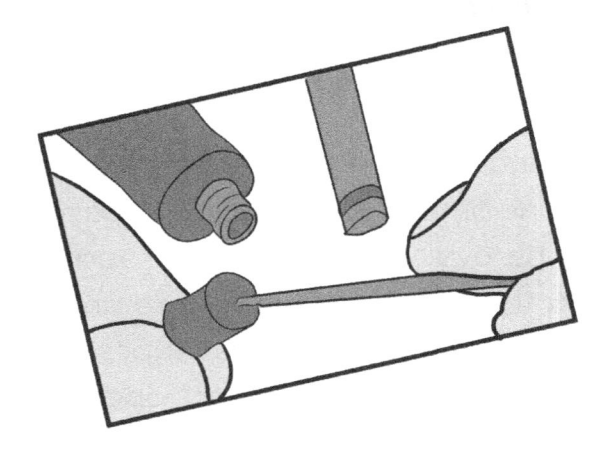

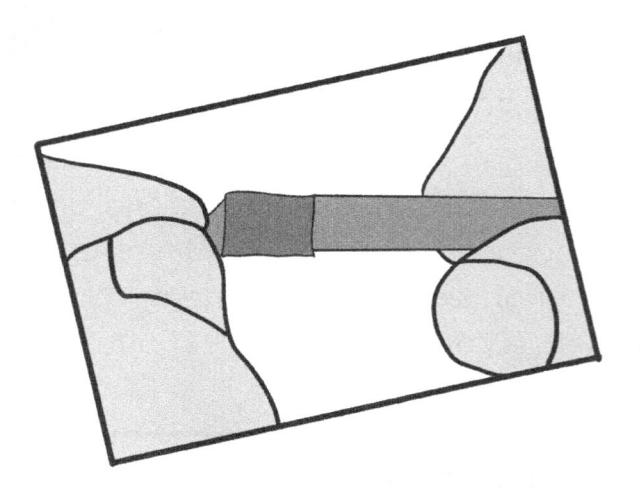

2. Rub a little glue along the inside surface of the end cap using a cotton bud, then apply a drop or two inside at the end. Avoid putting a stain on the finding outside.

3. Force the braid (or cords) into your end cap, ensuring it's flat and no rough edges are dangling; you should use the costume designer's pin to fasten any leftover fibers inside. Redo the same with the other end and leave it to dry for a day.

Attach a Loop to an End Cone or Cap

Some end cone or cap types have a hole at their edges, instead of a rim. You can connect a piece of string or a headpin to the braid and then make a wrapped or simple loop. Use the style to match the procedure, so that the bare ends are hidden, and the end cap or cone edge securely wraps around the cords or braid.

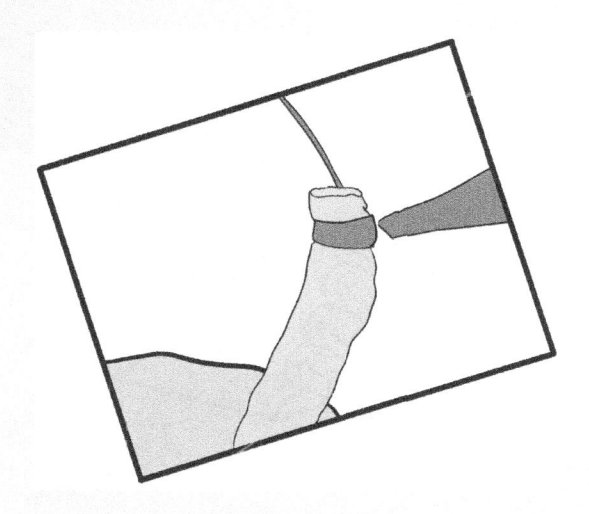

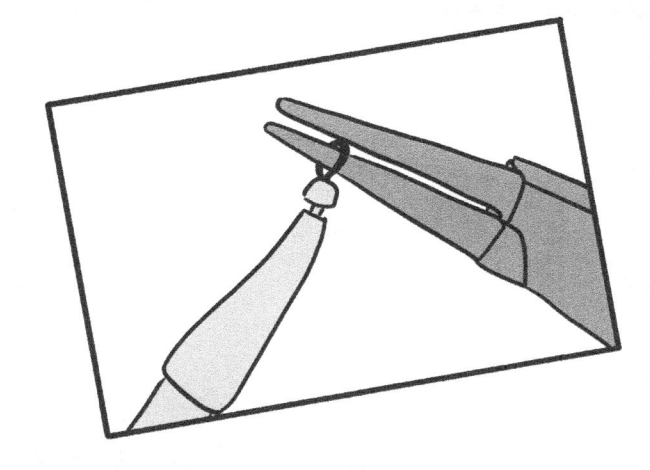

2. Carry the end of the headpin out into the middle of the braid edge. Use snipe-nose cutters to twist the headpin end back over the wrapping towards the braided end.

3. Add the glue within the end cap or cone and push the braid through the hole to feed the headpin.

4. Work a flat loop at the headpins end. If the hole is wide, you should add a tiny bead before making the circle, to fill the space.

Finishing Ends

The starting of macramé and other knotting methods is often connected with a string or into a fastening, and there are no bare edges. Even so, the working end has still ended to complete. If the structure allows, you may leave a fringe, or users may use several other finishing techniques.

Gluing the Ends

Some glues dry out and become brittle, but jewelry glue will remain malleable once dry for a much safer and more

PAGE 53

durable join.

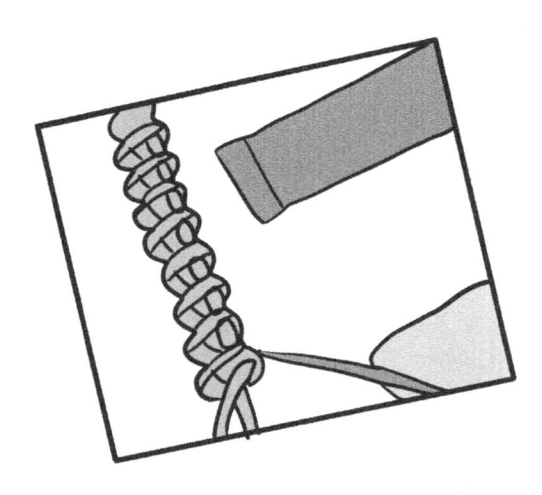

1. Use a cocktail stick or a fine-nozzle glue tube to add a thin adhesive under the end cords (EC) where it appears from the last knot. Put on to dry for 24 hours.

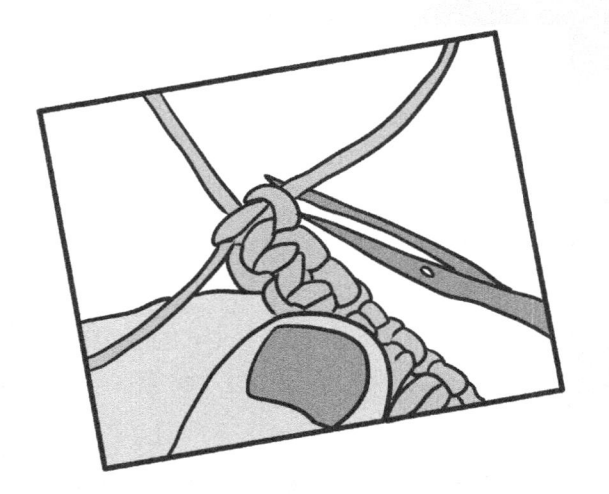

2. Ensure the ends of the cord are protected. For wax cotton cords (WCC) trim the strands closer to the knot.

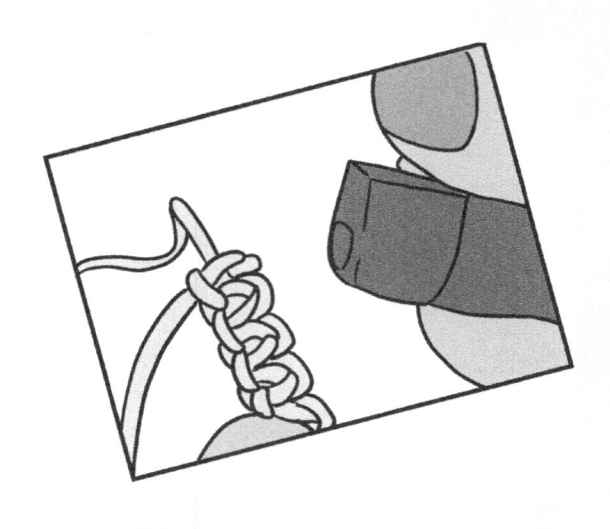

3. Using a nylon string, such as a Chinese knotting rope, cut a little more and now melt the end cautiously with a small lighter.

Tip: Do not use superglue or gel instantaneously (cyanoacrylate), because these can go tough and crack over time.

TYING KNOTS

Often a basic overhand knot is sufficed to neaten the ends of the string, or you may attempt the wider and more elaborate double variety.

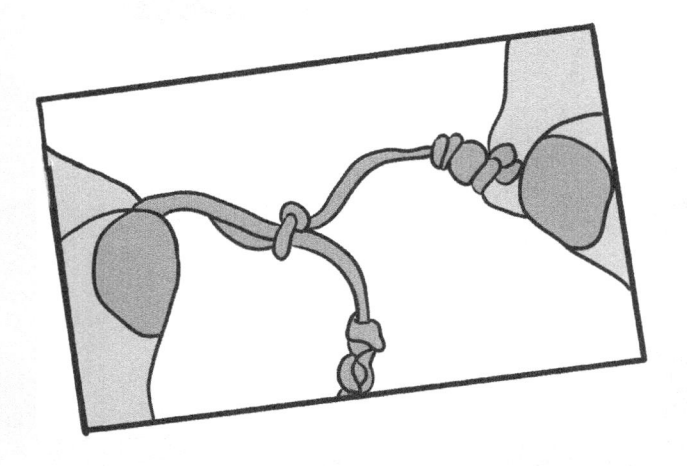

Overhand Knot

1. Making an overhand knot to the end of the string will avoid breakage and neaten it. Adding a bead before working your knot provides a beautiful finish.

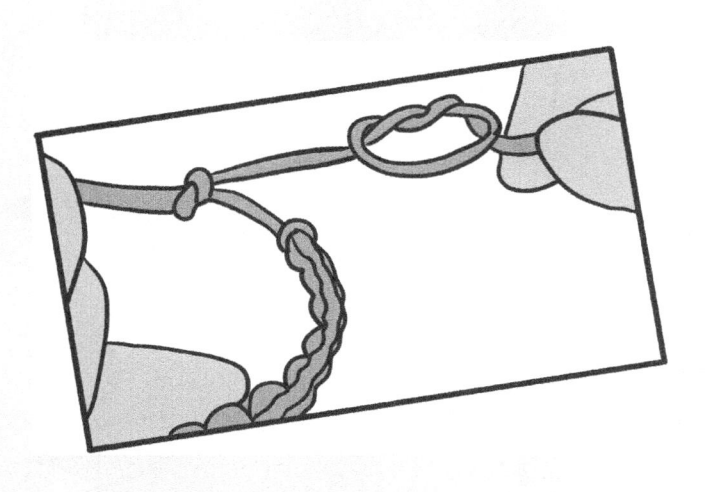

Double Overhand Knot (DOK)

1. Start by putting an overhand knot (OK), now take the working end (WE) through the loop one more time.

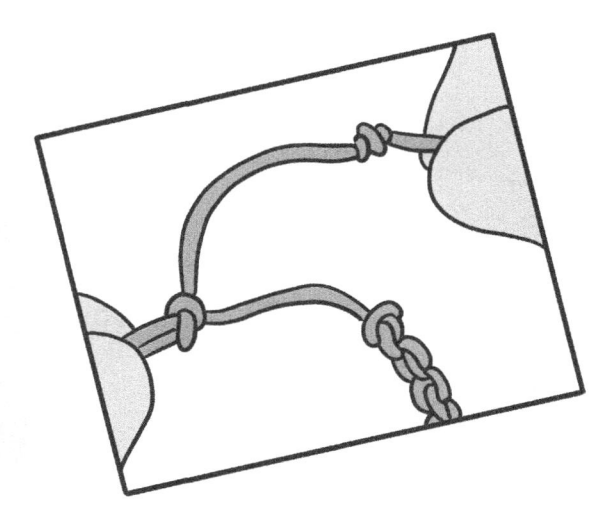

2. Pull either end to make the knot secure, readjust it while you secure the knot if needed. Add a drop of glue and cut.

PAGE 55

CORD FASTENINGS

Fastening can be created using a macramé or knotting strings, from a plain sliding fastening with overhand knots (OK) to the more ornate Chinese button knot (CBK) with its toggle and loop.

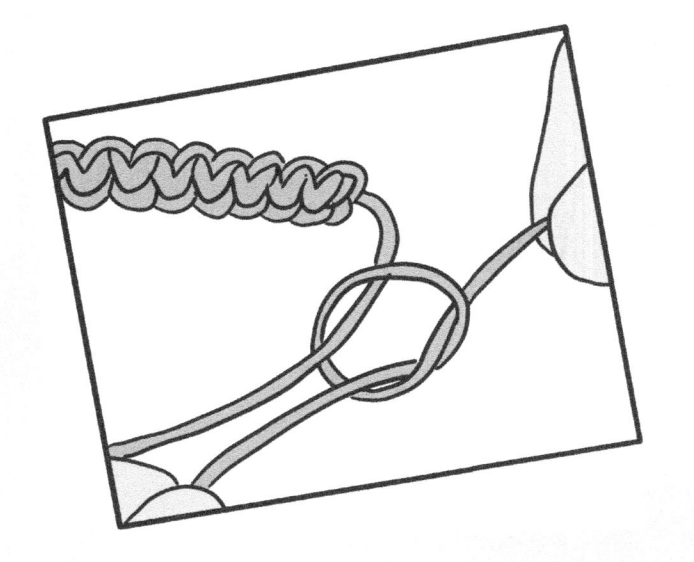

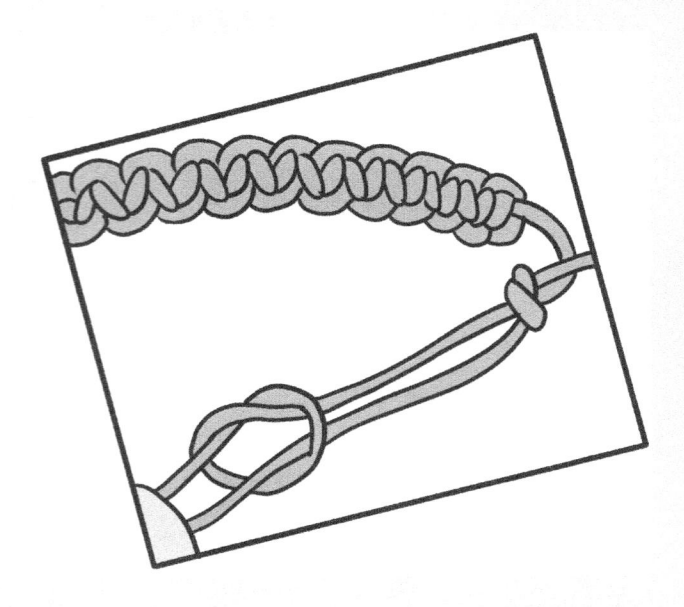

2. Redo using the other end to tie an overhand knot (OK). Pull those pretty tight strings until they cannot move.

Chinese Button Knot (CBK)

Sliding Knot (SK) Fastening

1. Place the bracelet cord parallel, but in opposite directions, to create a quick slide fastener. Hook one end of an overhand knot (OK) over the other string.

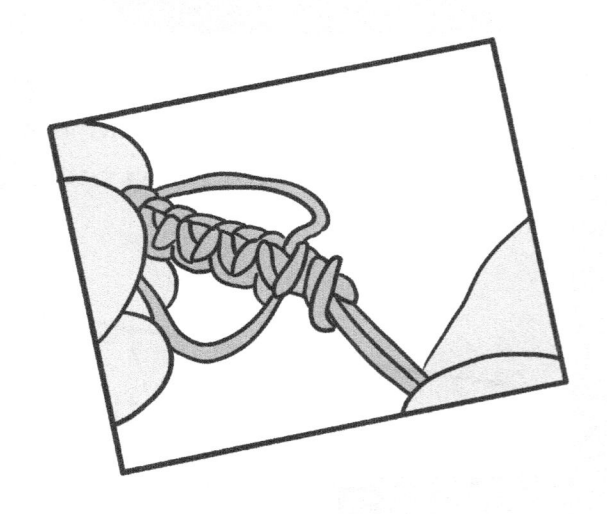

1. Work up to the length of the braid needed to allow the toggle-and-loop fastening. Attach the two core cords (CC) together in an overhand knot (OK) near the knotting, apply a bit of glue

and shave the excess ends.

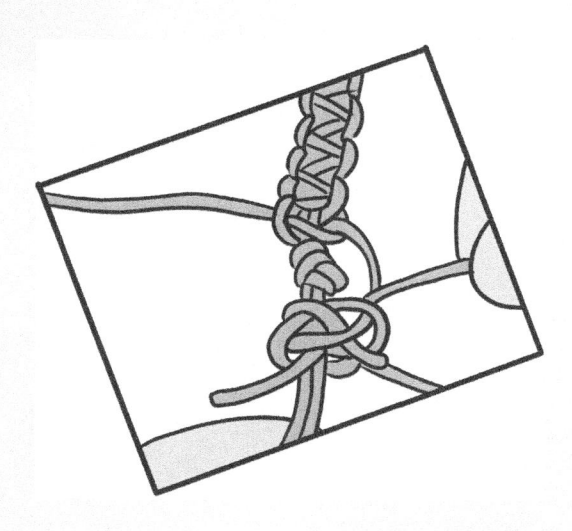

2. Use one of your side strings to tie a knot around the central cords (CC) to make a toggle.

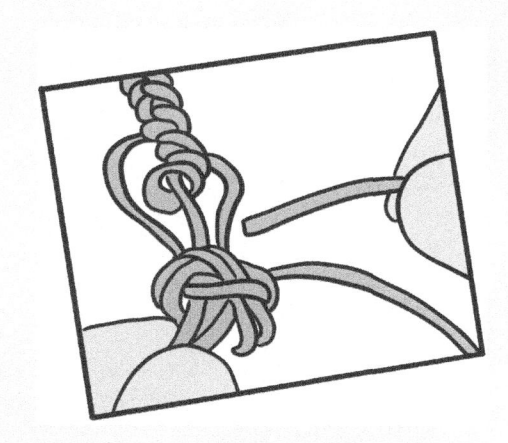

3. Thread the other side cord around the edge of your toggle to make a double-strand knot (DSK). Carry all side cords out before tightening up at the top of the knot.

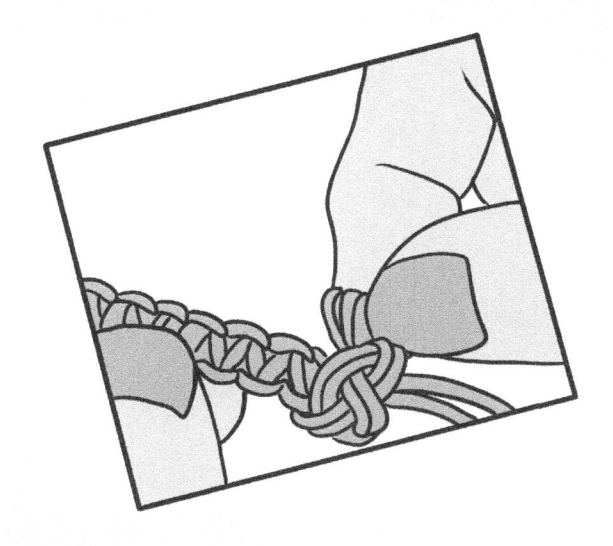

4. Take the loops one at a time and work around become to keep the knot secure so that it wraps around the overhand knot (OK), next to the end of the rope. Apply a small amount of adhesive where the cords started, then either shave or heat up the ends to complete, shaping the ball to hide the ends.

For this bright and colorful key charm, the Chinese button knot toggle fastening was used.

Chapter 5

MACRAMÉ TROUBLESHOOTING

I would like to share the most common mistakes in doing macramé projects and how to fix them. They are as follows:

ERROR 1

When tying a knot, do it in a sloppy way.

How to fix:

1. Hold the cord under the 6 inches mark (junction) with your left hand and the cord end facing upward on top of your right hand.

2. Bend both hands inward, making sure the cords are at the same level and are under pressure before tying the knot as shown in the picture.

3. Pull on both ends of the cord to tighten the knot before cutting off the excess part of both cords.

ERROR 2

Not making the cord longer when making a knot.

How to fix:

1. Keep tension on the knot, 1 to 2 inches higher than the knot itself.

2. Pull on both ends of the cord to pull it in, this will reduce any stress caused by the knot, resulting in more durability for your cord and fastening knots well.

ERROR 3

Not using enough tension while tying knots and cords together.

How to fix:

1. When tying a new cord to an existing rope, tighten it under pressure, don't let it flop around loosely.

2. When adding another loop of cord to an existing rope, make sure that you pull fairly hard on all ends of both cords before joining them together.

3. When adding one or more cords to an existing cord, regulate the pressure so that both cords are always under equal tension.

ERROR 4

Not using the right type of knot for a certain macramé project

How to fix:

1. Using a granny knot for decorative purposes only and not for fastening rope together.

2. Using a lark's head knot for an 8-in-1 or 6-in-1 when you should have used an overhand knot.

3. Using an overhand knot when you should have used an overhand loop knot.

4. And many others too.

Chapter 6
HOW TO DO A BUSINESS WITH MACRAMÉ

HOW CAN YOU PREVENT MAKING MACRAMÉ MISTAKES?

- Read and understand the instructions carefully before starting a project.

- Important: Do all the knots slowly and carefully, don't be in a hurry or just "wing it."

- Be enduring with yourself, this is not some kind of race, so take your time to do things properly and neatly.

- Similarly, it helps if you have somebody who is experienced in macramé nearby to assist whenever you get stuck in doing a certain knot or technique.

- Lastly, to keep a positive attitude in doing projects. Any time you find yourself getting frustrated with how a project is going, stop, walk away, and take a break from it. You can at all times come back to it later and start again when you're calm again. Remember, this is not something that you finish overnight, nor should you pressure yourself into finishing it as fast as possible since the end result will be more satisfying when done properly and neatly.

SELLING MACRAMÉ ITEMS ON ETSY SUCCESSFULLY

Here, I will detail the enormous pieces of how to sell adequately on Etsy, from making that especially critical relationship with buyers, to ensuring potential customers find your things.

As you read this part, review managing your Etsy postings and promoting them as just a single piece of a productive, skilled worker business.

At the point when the orders are coming in, you must get the items to your customers quickly and viably. Etsy is an immense stage for promoting and selling your creative works.

Etsy gives a far-reaching stage to selling things and draws a large buying gathering of observers searching for exceptional works. Making your things stand unique and different from others is the best approach to advance on Etsy, and this requires consistent effort. So before bouncing into how to sell on Etsy, it's essential to guarantee that selling on Etsy is right for you.

Here are 3 questions you should ask yourself:

- **Do I have the crucial specific aptitudes to sway Etsy?** It's noteworthy to have, at any rate, a critical working learning of taking, changing, and transferring product photos, getting and sending messages, and investigating site pages and drop-down menus. Etsy is exceptionally natural and amazingly expedient to use once you get the hang of its dashboard. In any case, there's a desire to learn and adjust on the off chance that you're new to electronic selling.

- **Do my products fit Etsy's most gainful worth point?** There are a ton of viable Etsy shops whose everyday product sells for upwards of $50. Etsy's editors understand that lower costs get a more significant number of clients. So, they viably search for vendors with esteem pointers under $50 to include in their ever-standard Editor's Picks portions.

- **Am I ready to put aside the push to do most of the course of action, passing on, and packaging/dispatching Etsy requirements?** Doing works, posting, and advancing them on Etsy, tending to buyer questions, and finally squeezing and conveying things all require effort, despite low support concern. Selling on Etsy requires some different options from posting things on a page and crossing your fingers.

MAKE A CONNECTION WITH YOUR BUYERS

Bit-by-bit guidelines to sell on Etsy—make a brand. Regardless of how unique your product is, it's practically sure that others on Etsy are selling something equivalent. Taking everything into account, how might you separate yourself and convince customers to pick your products over other sellers? The proper reaction is stamping.

STUNNING PHOTOS

In about a moment, a horrible photograph or debilitating product depiction can wreck all the constant work you put into working up your items and brand. Since you understand how to connect with your clients, the following stage is to focus on displaying your products in the best light. Photographs are the principal way a potential customer can envision works and check the idea of your products. Henceforth, incredible photos are in fact the most remarkable piece of the product presentation and an essential piece of making sense of how to sell on Etsy.

Etsy allows you to use five photos with each posting. You may require these to highlight everything about your creative works. Regardless, the images that you use ought to be staggering on the off chance that you might want to find accomplishment in selling on Etsy.

MAKE INTERESTING AND ACCURATE ITEM DESCRIPTIONS

Your product portrayal is your opportunity to attract potential customers and bait them to buy verbally. Approach your depictions as an informative conversation. You must give vital product information yet do it in an attractive and captivating tone.

HAVE FAST AND APPROACHABLE CORRESPONDENCE WITH BUYERS

Buyers will send you messages with various requests and offers, so keep checking your Etsy message box. It's basic to respond to these messages within one business day or less. This deftness passes on a sentiment of a clear strategy and besides, lets the customer know that you value their time and potential business.

Now, it is time to learn how to make various home decors—simply by using the art of macramé! Check them out and see which ones you want to make yourself!

Chapter 7

MACRAMÉ PLANT HANGERS AND HOME DÉCOR

1. MODERN MACRAMÉ HANGING PLANTER

Plant hangers are really beautiful because they give your house or garden the feel of an airy, natural space. This one is perfect for condominiums or small apartments—and those with minimalist, modern themes!

Materials

- **Plant**
- **Pot**
- **Scissors**
- **50 ft. Paracord (Parachute Cord)**
- **6 to 20 mm. wooden beads**

Instructions

1. First, fold in half 4 strands of the cord and then loop so you could form a knot.

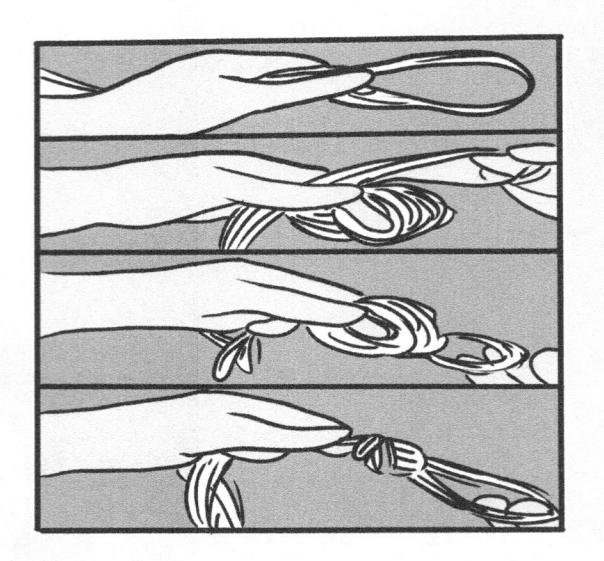

2. Now, divide the cords into groups of two, and make sure to string 2 cords through one of the wooden beads you have on hand. String some more beads—at least 4 on each set of 2 grouped cords.

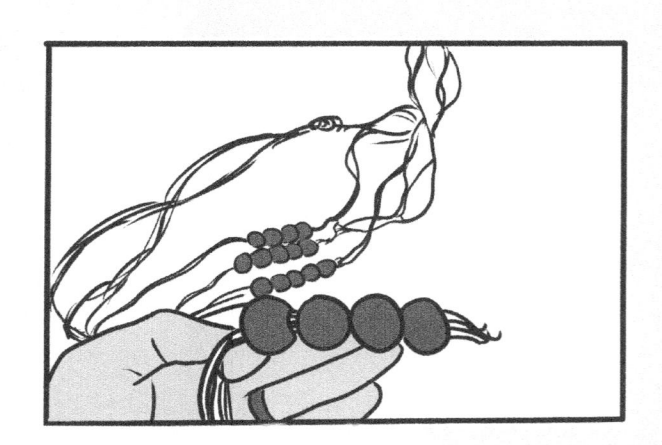

3. Then, measure every 27.5 inches and tie a knot at that point and repeat this

process for every set of cords.

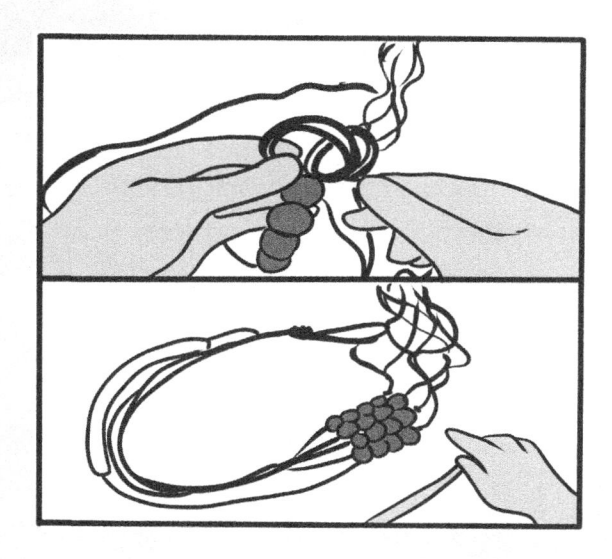

4. Look at the left set of the cord and tie it to the right string. Repeat on the four sets so that you could make at least 3 inches from the knot you have made.

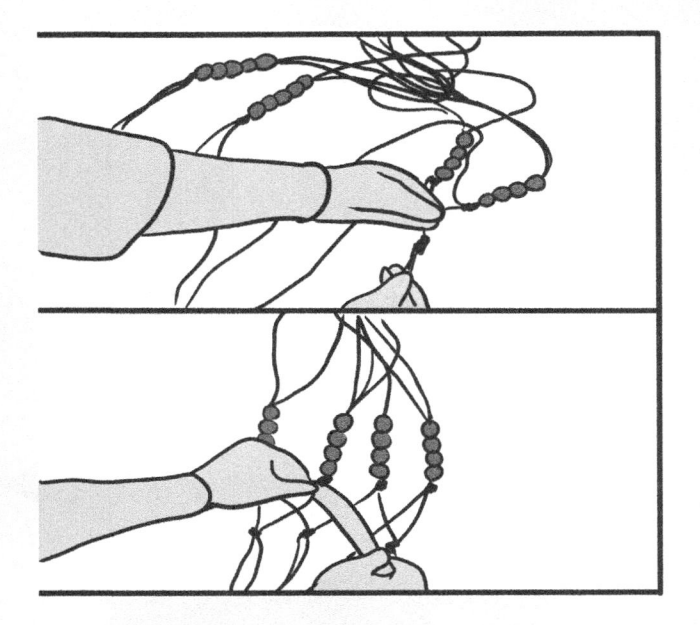

5. Tie another four knots from the knot that you have made. Make them at least 4.5 inches each.

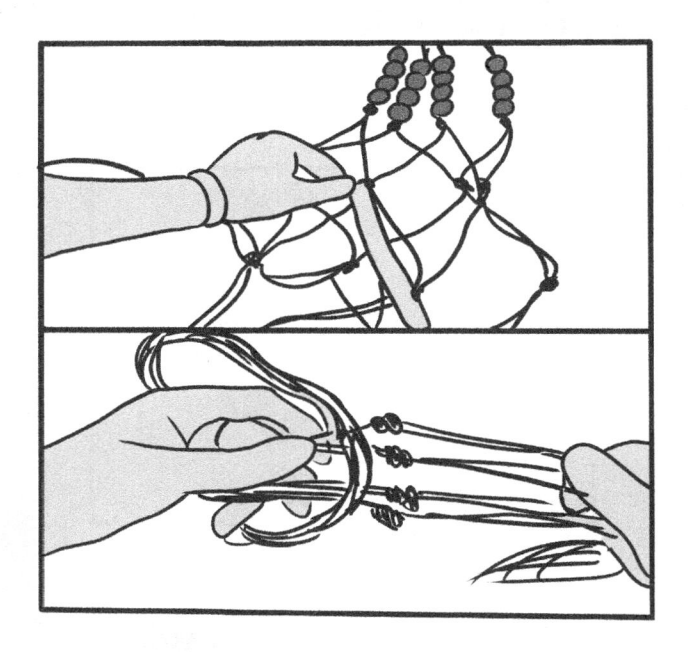

6. Group all of the cords together and tie a knot to finish the planter. You'll get something like the one shown below—and you could just add your very own planter to it!

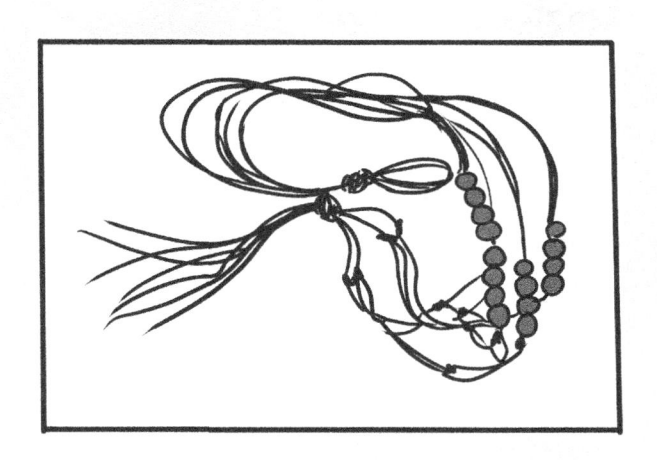

PAGE 67

2. MINI MACRAMÉ PLANTERS

Succulents are all the rage these days because they are just so cute and are really decorative! What's more, you can make a lot of them and place them around the house—that will definitely give your place a unique look!

Materials

- **Small container**
- **Garden soil/potting mix**
- **Succulents/miniature plants**
- **¼ inch jump ring**
- **8 yards of embroidery thread or thin cord**

Instructions

1. Cut 3.6 inches of 8 lengths of cord. Make sure that 1.8 inches are already enough to cover enough half-hitches. If not, you can always add more. Let the thread loop over the ring and then tie a wrap knot that could hold all the cords together.

2. Create a half-twist knot by tying half of a square knot and repeating it multiple times with the rest of the cord.

3. Drop a quarter inch of the cord down and repeat the step twice.

4. Arrange your planter and place it on the hanger that you have made.

5. Nail to the wall and enjoy seeing your mini-planter!

Chapter 8
CHRISTMAS PROJECTS

3. BOHO CHRISTMAS TREE

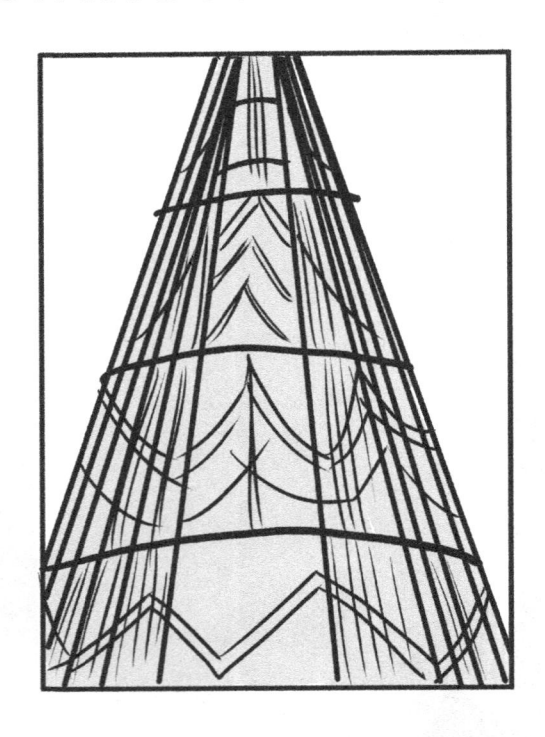

Materials

gardeA few branches or branches of the parts Wire of jewelry or other ornamental

- **A brush**
- **Fishing line hanging**

Instructions

1. Break the yarn into 7 to 8 inches sections. Take two threads, and fold half of them as a loop. Place a loop under a twig.

2. Take the looped end of the other beam and move the ends of the beam under the twig into the loop. Connect the thread under the twig at the ends of the rope.

3. Once enough knotted strands are inserted, separate the threads with a brush or comb. The "almost finished" tree is a little week so you have to stabilize it with some starch.

4. Cut them into a triangle and adorn them with small baubles or beads when the boho trees are high. I just made a little flower star joystick.

5. It takes about 10 minutes for a whole bunch to produce. I think they would make perfect presents or on your Christmas tree, you could hang them.

4. MINI MACRAMÉ CHRISTMAS ORNAMENTS

Materials

- **Macramé cord**
- **Hardness**
- **Blueberry or peanut**
- **Masking tape**
- **Scissors**
- **Get the twig cords**

Instructions

1. Cut a little twig in the beginning and use the lark's knot to tie 6 cords to the end.

2. How do you build a lark knot in 4 steps?

3. To tie a knot of a lark, first, fold it halfway and lie down over the top of the twig in the center.

4. Bend the loop over the back of the twig and pull both ends up. Pull close. Pull strong All 6 cords repeat.

5. First-knot square. The first chain, which is three square knots, must be started once the strings are on the twig. These knots are connected to four cords so that the first four cords begin to be divided on the left.

How to tie a square knot in four measurements to macramé?

6. To make the square knot, pull out the left cord to look like a "4" number.

7. Then tuck under the fourth string at the end of the first string.

8. So, pick up the end of the 4th cord and pick the gap between the first and second cord that looks like the four.

9. Tighten the 1st and 4th thread ends and move the nudge to the tip.

How to tie a square knot in a macramé college?

10. So, do the same thing for the second half of the square knot, but in the other direction. You form the 4 cords with the first and fourth cords but with the 4 cords on the right side.

11. Take the 4th first string.

12. Then feed into the 2nd and third strings the 1st string tail and into the 4th shape through the opening.

13. Tighten the 1st and 4th thread ends, and you've got the first square knot.

14. 1 to 3 degrees.

Steps to tie a knot in macramé:

15. Make four pieces of cord working. Keep another square knot and another square knot in the top row.

16. For the second section, you can only make 2 square knots. The first is divided into cords to do this. The second knot in row 2 will be followed by the next four cords. On the other hand, the other two cords are still left.

17. Use the four-string center of a row just to form a square knot for the third row.

18. You can change the stress, try to keep your knots twisted and evenly spaced. Four or five rows.

19. Small knot macramé, taped to a table.

20. Repeat row 2 for row 4 with 2 square knots, leaving both cords at the ends.

21. Repeat row 1 for row 5 with 3 knots square.

22. Line 6 half hook knot.

23. Take the first string and move the part horizontally to the half-knot. It will be your lead thread.

24. Take the second cord from behind the lead and through the hole you made. Now make the same knot again with the same 2nd thread. This is half a jump. It is a half jump.

25. Continue through the rest of the strings so that the lead cord is pulled through the other cords horizontally and directly.

26. To save the knots, push the lead thread.

Finishing of the decoration:

27. Cut the ends directly into a "V" down or up on the base to complete.

28. Then wear a hairbrush or a comb to brush the cord and build the fringe edge. Once you smooth it off, you can have to change the shape a little.

29. Cut the twig ends, then add a piece of string to hang the ornament up.

5. 7-POINT SNOWFLAKE

Materials

- 1 1.5 inches ring
- Any household clear-drying glue or fabric
- 2 mm. or 1.4 yards of white cord material
- Project board and pins

Instructions

1. All the cords should be mounted to the 1.5 inches ring with LHK. It can be done by folding the cord and placing it under the ring, then bring the ends over the front of the ring and down. The ends should be passed over the folded area. A reverse half hitch should also be tied, passing the ends under and over the ring and under the cord. All the other cords should go through this step, and at the end of this step; the cords should be organized into a group of 7 having four cords. All the knots should be well-tightened so that they won't loosen later on.

2. Two SK should be tied with each group of four cords. The fillers should also be pulled to firmly tighten them; this ensures that the first rests against the knots that are on the ring.

3. The four cords from the two SK should be numbered. The cords should be alternated by using cords 3 to 4 from an SK and using cords 1 to 2 from the other SK. At this juncture, one must be careful in selecting the four cords that come from the two adjacent knots while tying the ASK in a circle or ring.

4. The other cords should also follow step 3 to complete the second row

5. The cords should be alternated again so

that the same group is used as is done in step 2. The third row of the ASK should be tied all the way around the 7-point snowflake. Ensure that the knots in this row are ½ inch beneath the knots from the second row.

6. A picot has been made beneath each of the knots of step 5 using the four cords we just did. Now, let's get back to business. An SK should be tied below one of the knots that were tied in row three.

7. We need to make sure the knot rests against the one tied in step 5 above, so we move the knot up allowing it to form two picot loops

8. Still, with those same four cords, we will tie another SK that is close to the one that was recently tied. Before tightening the knots, glue should be applied to the fillers. Once the glue gets dried, the ends should be trimmed to 1 inch, and a fringe should be formed by separating the fibers at the ends of the 7-point snowflake

9. Steps 6 to 8 should be repeated with another set of cords.

10. There is a higher percentage that the knots may loosen as time goes on if a cotton cable cord is being used and although this is an optional step, it is also advised. The snowflake can be turned over, and fabric glue should be applied behind each knot. Another thing to take note of about the fabric glue to be used is that it must be such that it dries clear.

Chapter 9
PERSONAL PROJECTS

6. HEART KEYCHAIN

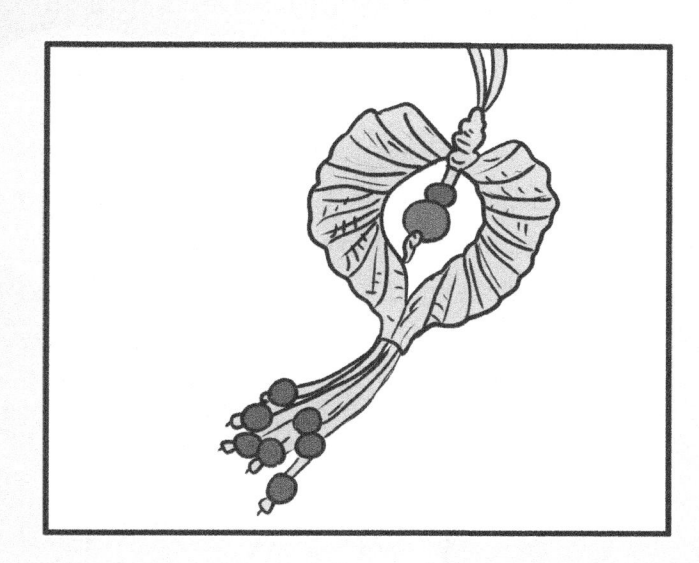

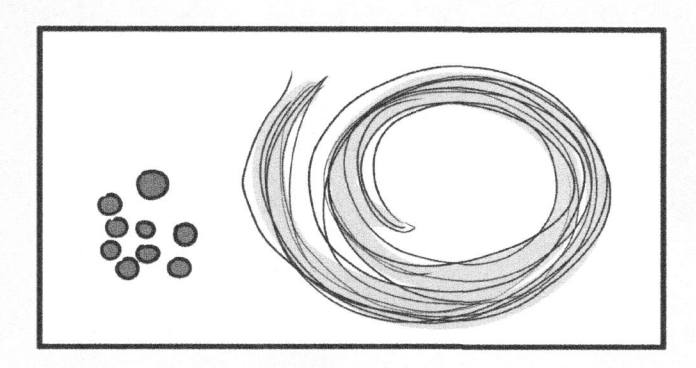

Materials
- 8 smaller beads
- 1 big bead
- 8 threads each 2.7 inches long

Instructions

1. You will be making an overhand knot. Take one thread, fold it in half, and now form a loop on top of the folded thread. This can be done by using your thumb as a guide to how long the loop should be. Then hold the thread at this length so that the loop is isolated.

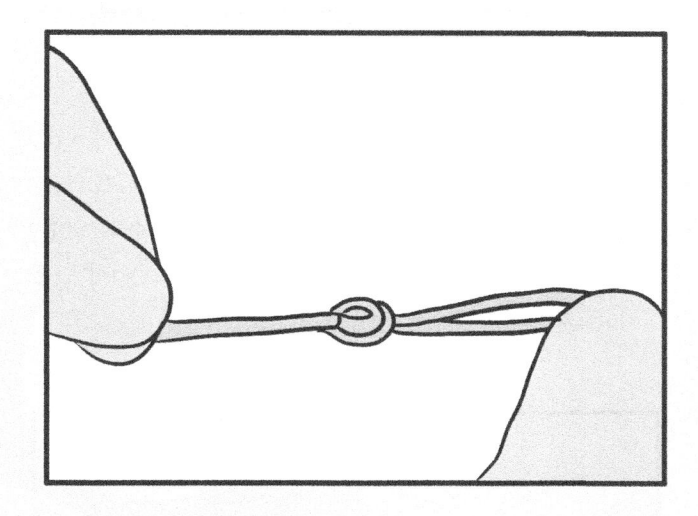

2. Whilst keeping the loop isolated, create another loop with the rest of the thread and then place the original loop through the new loop while keeping hold of the original loop and then when through you can pull to tighten and you should end up with something like the picture below. This is what your overhand knot should look like.

PAGE 77

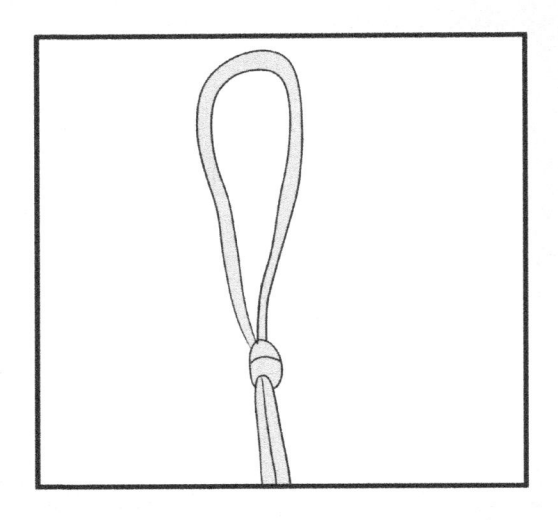

hand thread. Simultaneously, pull the threads on the left and right side so that it tightens, and a knot is created.

5. Take the single thread on the right, laid it over the two threads in the middle and under the left thread. Now take the left thread under the two threads in the middle and under the loop created on the right. Pull to tighten (both sides at the same time) and create your knot.

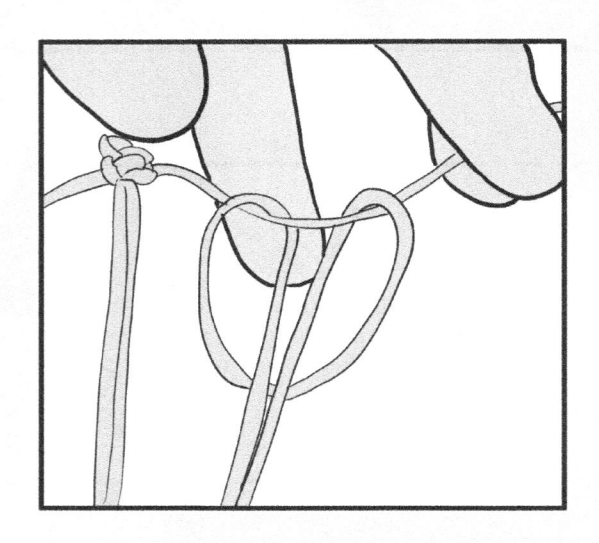

3. Take another one of your threads, and place it over your previous thread with the knot in it ensuring that the knot is in the middle of the new thread you have just chosen.

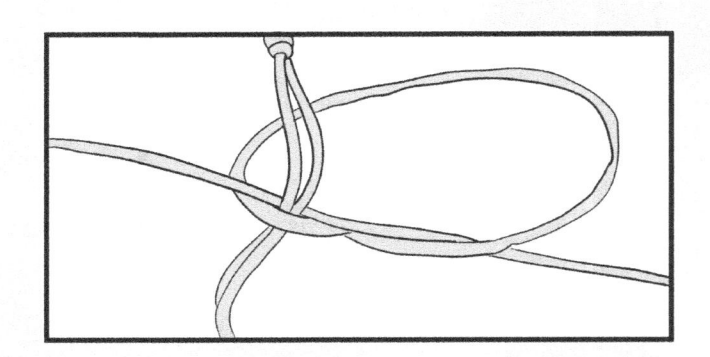

4. Now you are going to tie a square knot. Take the left-hand side of the thread that you have just laid down (the one without the knot) and place it over the thread above it and under the thread on the right. Then take the right-side thread and thread it under the thread at the bottom and under the left-hand side and through the loop that has been created by the left-

6. Take the single thread on the left, then take the single thread on the right. Ensure that both threads are horizontal. For now, you will only be working with the right so you can set the left side down until later.

7. Take a new single thread and fold it in half, make sure there is a loop created at the top. Then place the thread behind the single thread on the right and fold over the top. Now, pull the two

loose threads through the middle of the loop so that it looks as above. Then pull the threads so that the thread tightens, and you will end up with a Lark's head knot.

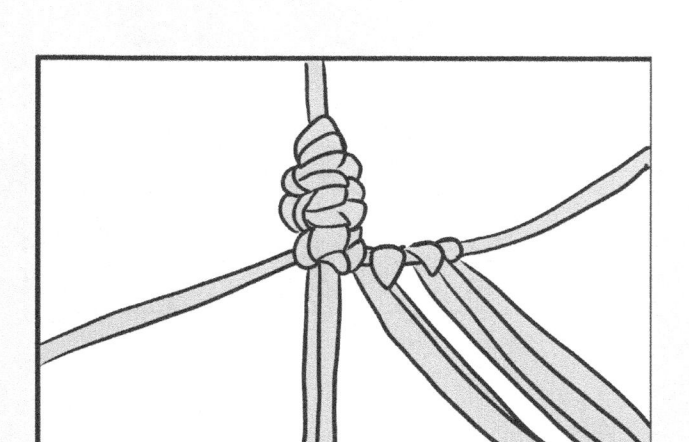

8. Take two more single threads and repeat step 7 until you end up with two more Lark's head knots on the right.

9. Take the left single thread, which should be horizontal as stated earlier. Then create three more Lark's head knots on the left single thread. It should look like the picture above.

10. Now you should have three lark's head knots on each side.

11. You should now have two threads in the middle. Take a small bead and thread it onto the two threads.

12. Take a big bead and place it on the same thread pushing it all the way to the top so that your macramé piece looks like the one in the picture.

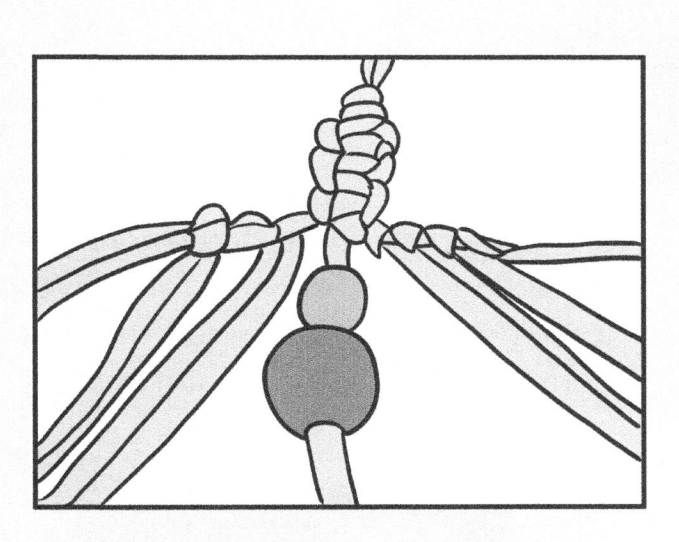

13. Tie a simple overhand knot at the end of the middle thread, under the beads, so that the beads are locked in place. There are instructions above on how to do this.

14. Take a pair of scissors and cut the loose thread at the end of the knot leaving just the knot. Refer to the image above.

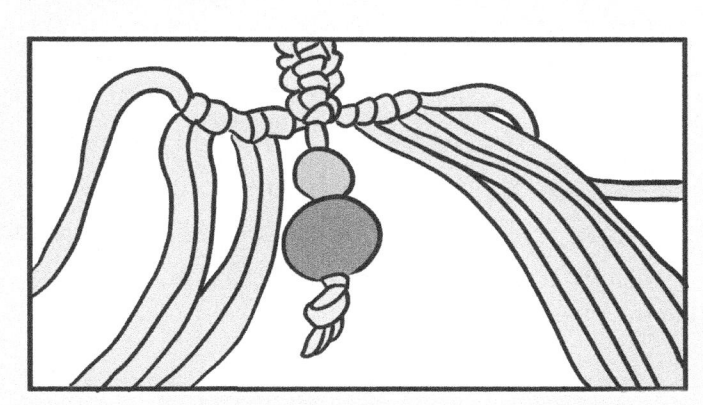

15. From your left group of threads, take the first on the right and place it horizontally across the other threads in the bunch. Then take the thread next to it, loop it over the horizontal thread, under itself, then using the same thread loop it over the horizontal thread again, and finally through the loop created. Pull to secure the knot tightly. You will have a hal-hitch knot.

16. Repeat this step with each thread until you all threads on the left have been done.

17. Take the next thread, directly under the half hitch knot, on the right. Pull this thread across horizontally and repeat the process of creating the half-hitch knot.

18. Repeat this process 6 more times so you have 8 half-hitch knots in total like the picture below. (excluding the one at the bottom)

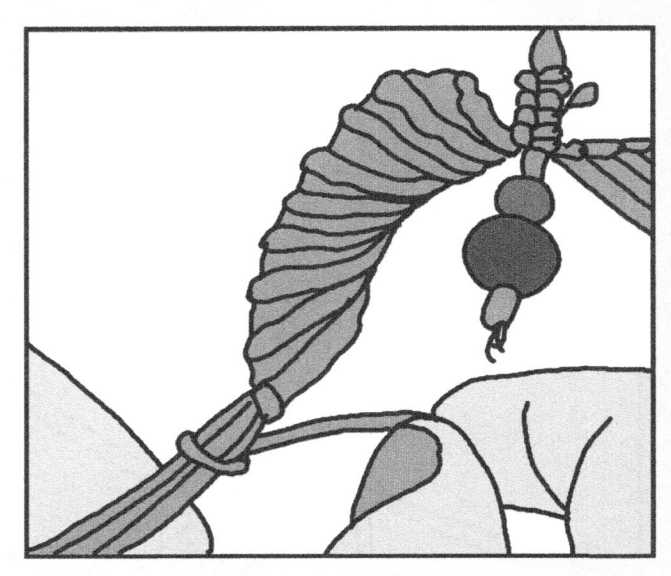

19. Here you will be creating the knot at the bottom of the left side.

20. Take the first thread on the right of the bottom knot. Then take the thread next to it, loop it over the horizontal thread, under itself, then using the same thread loop it over the horizontal thread again, and finally through the loop created. Pull to secure the knot tightly. You will have a half-hitch knot.

21. Take the thread used to create the hal-hitch knot and place it horizontally across the rest of the threads. Take the next thread and wrap it around both horizontal threads, under itself, then using the same threads loop them over the horizontal threads, and finally through the loop created. Pull to tighten

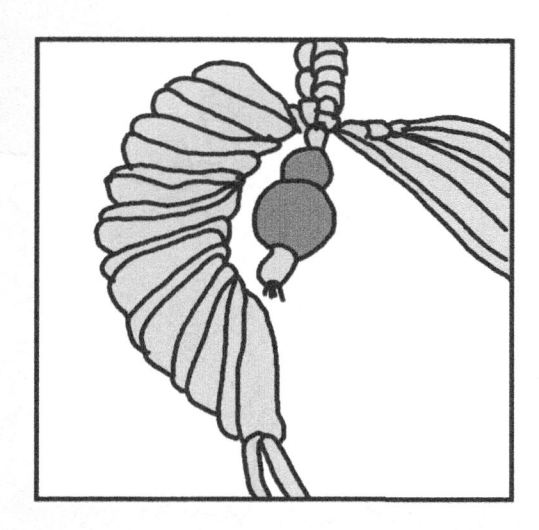

succeed.

22. Then take the thread just used for the horizontal thread and place it across the remaining threads. You should have three horizontal threads. Take the threads next to it and wrap them around the three horizontal threads to create a half-hitch knot. Take the next thread and wrap it around both horizontal threads, under itself, then using the same threads loop them over the horizontal threads, and finally through the loop created. Pull to tighten

23. Repeat this process, add one thread each time, until you get to the last thread. Your macramé piece should look like the image above.

24. This is what your finished left side should look like. If you have made any mistakes, it is okay to go back and change them. The last half hitch knot can be hard to follow but use the pictures to aid you and you will

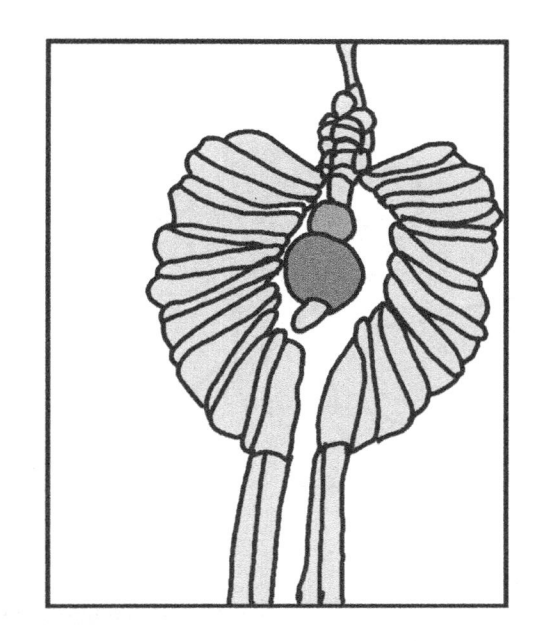

25. For the completion of the right side, start in the same way you did for the left side. This is exactly the same process and if you completed the left side, you shouldn't find it too hard. Repeat the steps given previously.

26. When completed it should look like the illustration given above. Don't worry if you don't get it the first time. You can always undo your stitching and try again.

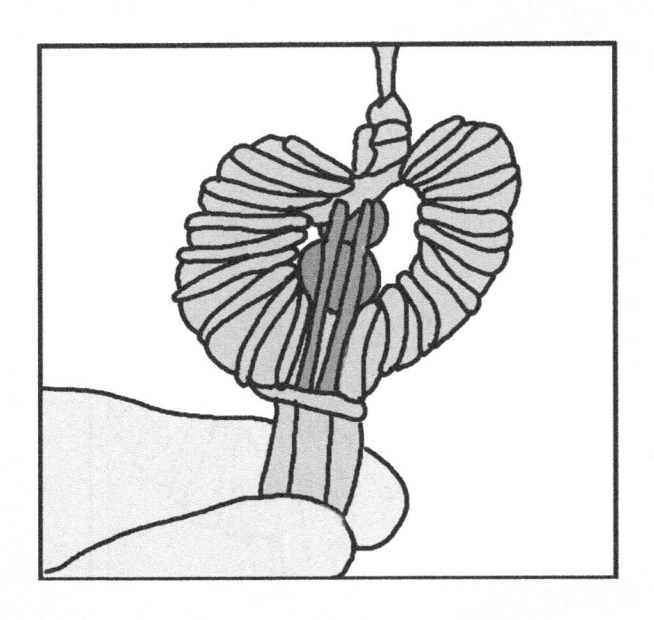

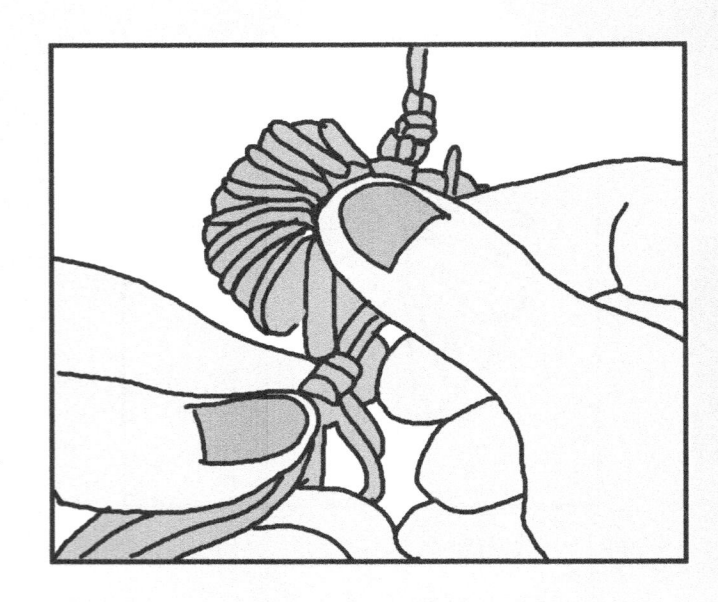

27. With the hanging threads from both the left and right sides, pull to make sure they are vertical. The threads should be together as one group.

28. Cut a piece of the thread, around 4 inches, and fold it in half to use. Now place this piece of thread in the middle of the bunch but sitting on top and the two ends facing the top as in the picture (purple thread).

29. Take a single thread from the group of threads. Wrap it around the group of threads as shown above.

30. Continue to wrap the thread around the group of threads until there is only a short portion of the single thread left. There should have been a loop created by the short piece of thread cut earlier (purple thread in photo). Place the end of the thread (purple) through the loop as shown, and pull the two ends of the loose thread (purple) at the top so that the loose thread (purple) will come out completely and the end of the single thread becomes trapped inside the loop creating a knot.

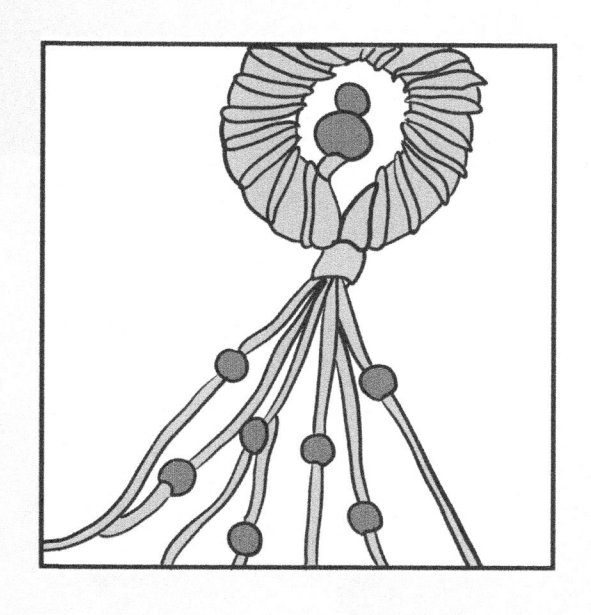

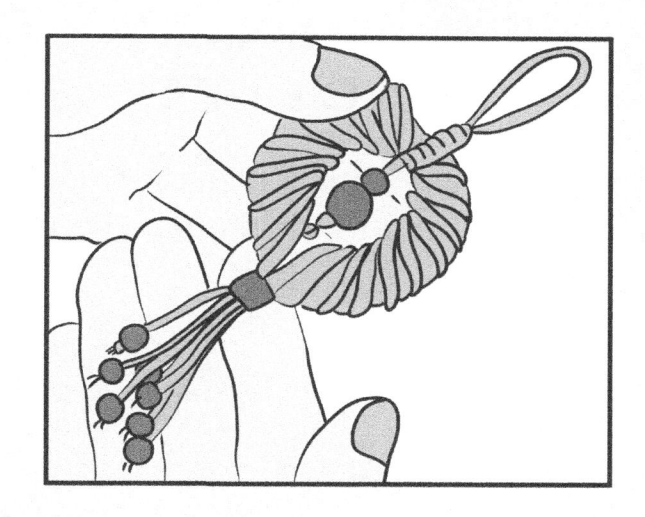

31. You should have several threads hanging loose from the knot just created. Place a small bead through each thread and show them to have the same intervals between them. They should be staggered creating the pattern shown.

32. Now do an overhand knot at the end of each bead to secure it in place. Refer to earlier instructions on how to complete this.

33. Trim the remaining threads from underneath the knots.

34. This is what your final macramé piece should look like. You will have a beautiful keychain to use yourself or gift to someone.

7. SERENITY BRACELET

(Note: if you are familiar with the flat knot, you can move right along into the next pattern)

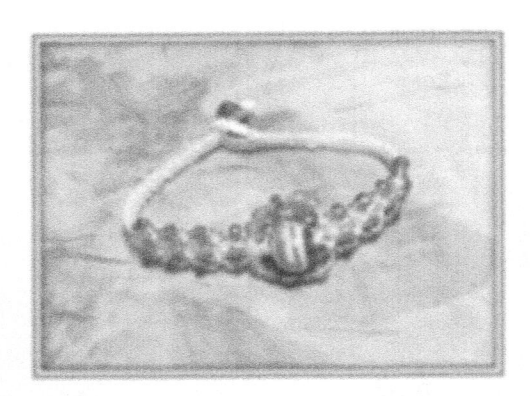

This novice bracelet offers plenty of practice using one of micro macramé's most used knots. You will also gain experience beading and equalizing tension. This bracelet features a button closure, and the finished length is 7 inches.

Materials

- **White C-Lon cord, 6 ½ ft., x 3**
- **18 frosted purple size 6 beads**
- **36 purple seed beads, size 11**
- **11 cm. purple and white focal bead**
- **26 dark purple size 6 beads**
- **1 to 5 mm. purple button closure bead (the button bead needs to be able to fit onto all 6 cords)**

Instructions

1. Take all 3 cords and fold them in half. Find the center and place it on your work surface as shown:

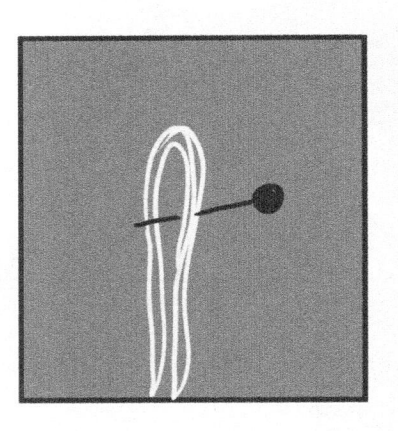

2. Now hold the cords and tie an overhand knot, loosely, at the center point. It should look like this:

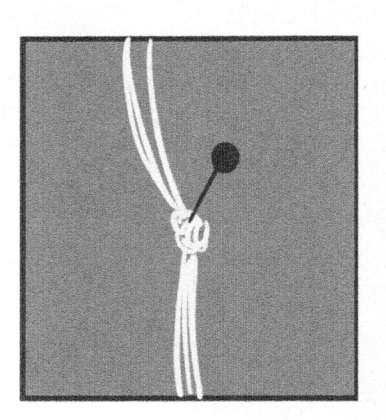

3. We will now make a buttonhole closure. Just below the knot, take each outer cord and tie a flat knot (aka square knot). Continue tying flat knots until you have about 2 ½ cm.

PAGE 84

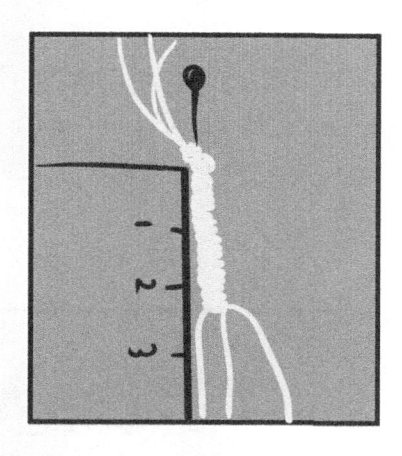

4. Undo your overhand knot and place the ends together in a horseshoe shape.

5. We now have all 6 cords together. Think of the cords as numbered 1 through 6 from left to right. Cords 2 to 5 will stay in the middle as filler cords. Find cords 1 and 6 and use these to tie flat knots around the filler cords. (Note: now you can pass your button bead through the opening to ensure a good fit. Add or subtract flat knots as needed to create a snug fit. This size should be fine for a 5 mm. bead). Continue to tie flat knots until you have 4 cm. worth.

(To increase bracelet length, add more flat knots here and the equal amount in step 10).

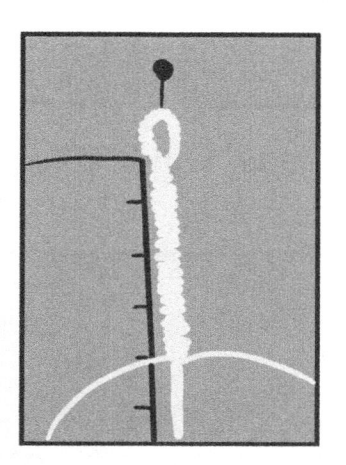

6. Separate cords 1, 4, and 1. Find the center 2 cords. Thread a size 6 frosted purple bead onto them, then tie a flat knot with cords 2 and 5.

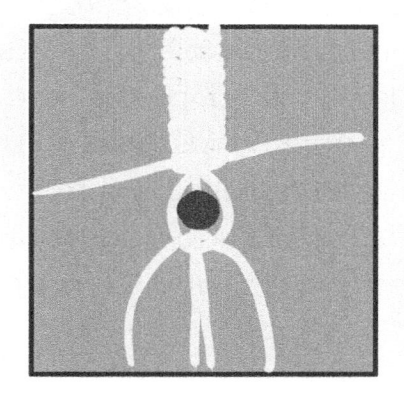

7. We will now work with cords 1 and 6. With cord 1 thread on a seed bead, a dark purple size 6 beads, and another seed bead. Repeat with cord 6, and then separate the cords into 3 and 3. Tie a flat knot with the left 3 cords. Tie a flat knot with the right 3 cords.

PAGE 85

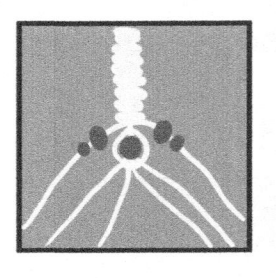

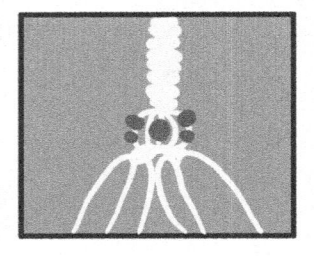

8. Repeat steps 4 and 5 three times.

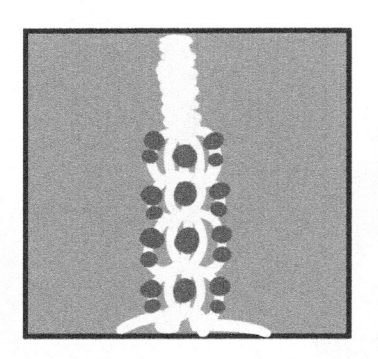

9. Find the center 2 cords, hold them together and thread on the 1 cm. focal bead. Take the next cords out (2 and 5) and bead as follows: 6 dark purple beads, 1 frosted purple bead, and 2 dark purple beads. Find cords 1 and 6 and bead as follows: 2 frosted purple beads, 1 seed bead, 1 dark purple bead, 1 seed bead, and 2 frosted purple beads.

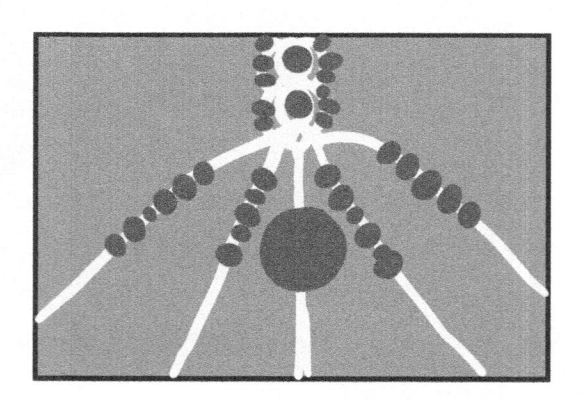

10. With cords 2 and 5, tie a flat knot around the center 2 cords. Place the center 4 cords together and tie a flat knot around them with outer cords 1 and 6.

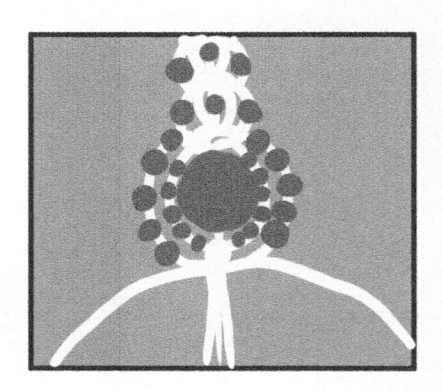

11. Repeat steps 4 and 5 four times.

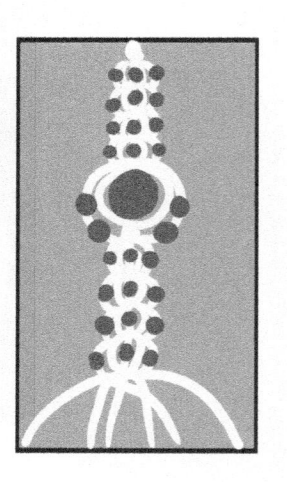

12. Repeat step 3.

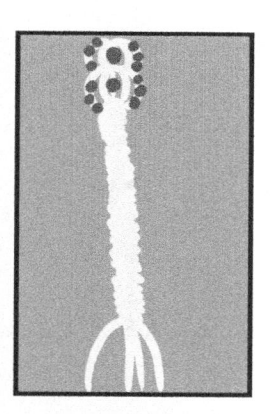

13. Place your button bead on all 6 cords and tie an overhand knot tight against the bead. Glue well and trim the cords.

8. LANTERN BRACELET

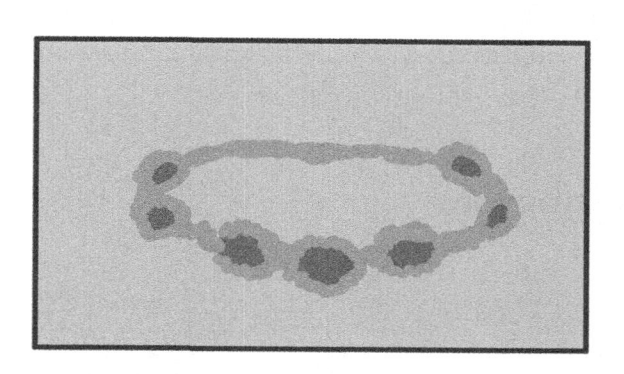

This pattern may look simple but please don't try it if you are in a hurry. This one takes patience. Don't worry about getting your picot knots all the exact same shape. Have fun with it! The finished bracelet is 7 ¼ inches in length. If desired, add a picot knot and a spiral knot on each side of the centerpiece to lengthen it. This pattern has a jump ring closure.

Materials
- **3 strands of C-Lon cord (2 light brown and 1 medium brown) 63 inches lengths**
- **Fasteners (1 jump ring, 1 spring ring, or lobster clasp)**
- **Glue Beacon 527 multi-uses**
- **8 small beads (about 4 mm.) amber to gold colors**
- **30 gold seed beads**
- **3 beads (about 6 mm.) of amber color (mine are rectangular, but round or oval**

will work wonderfully also)

Note: Bead size can vary slightly. Just be sure all beads you choose will slide onto 2 cords (except seed beads).

Instructions

1. Find the center of your cord and attach it to the jump ring with a lark's head knot. Repeat with the 2 remaining strands. If you want the 2-tone effect, be sure your second color is NOT placed in the center, or it will only be a filler cord and you will end up with a 1 tone bracelet.

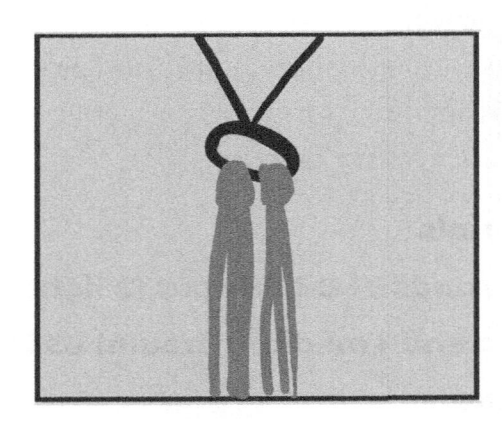

2. You now have 6 cords to work with. Think of them numbered 1 through 6, from left to right. Move cords 1 and 6 apart from the rest. You will use these to work the spiral knot. All others are filler cords. Take cord number 1 and tie a spiral knot. Always begin with the left cord. Tie 7 more spirals.

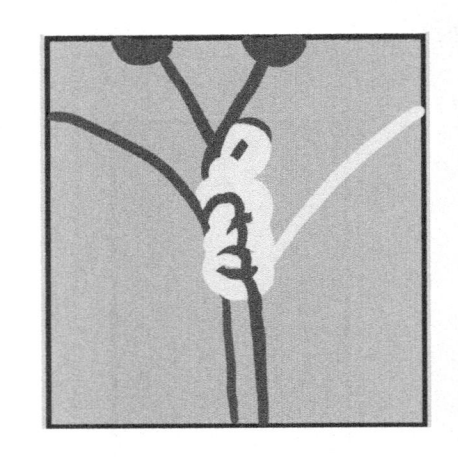

3. Place a 4 mm. bead on the center 2 cords. Leave cords 1 and 6 alone for now and work 1 flat knot using cords 2 and 5.

4. Now put cords 2 and 5 together with the center strands. Use 1 and 6 to tie a picot flat knot. If you don't like the look of your picot knot, loosen it up and try again. Gently tug the cords into place then lock them in tightly with the next spiral knot.

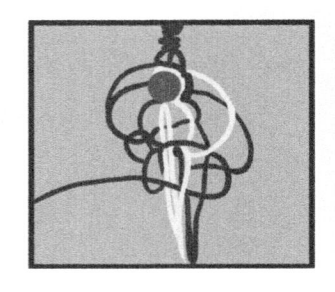

Notice here how I am holding the picot knot with my thumbs while pulling the cords tight with my fingers. If you look closely, you may be able to see that I have a cord in each hand.

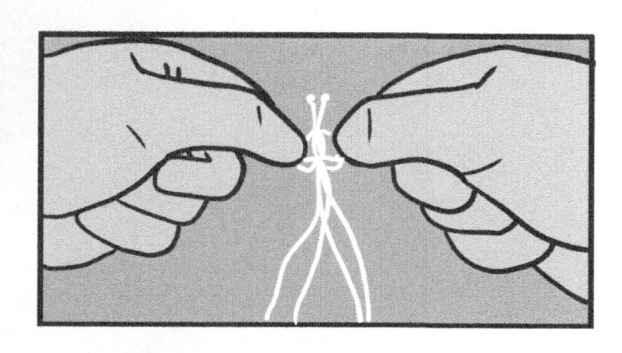

the outermost cords.

5. Tie 8 spiral knots (using the left cord throughout the pattern).

6. Place a 4 mm. bead on the center 2 cords. Leave cords 1 and 6 alone for now and work 1 flat knot using cords 2 and 5. Now put cords 2 and 5 together with the center strands. Use strands 1 and 6 to tie a picot flat knot.

7. Repeat steps 5 and 6 until you have 5 sets of spirals.

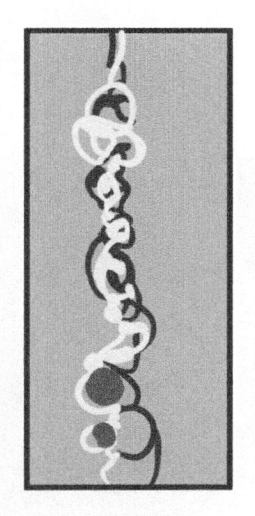

8. Next place 5 seed beads on cords 1 and 6. Put cords 3 and 4 together and string on a 6 mm. bead. Tie one flat knot with

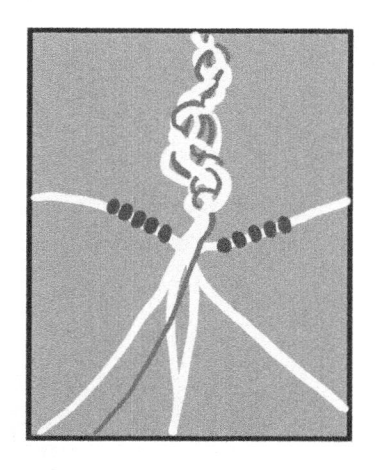

9. Repeat this step two more times.

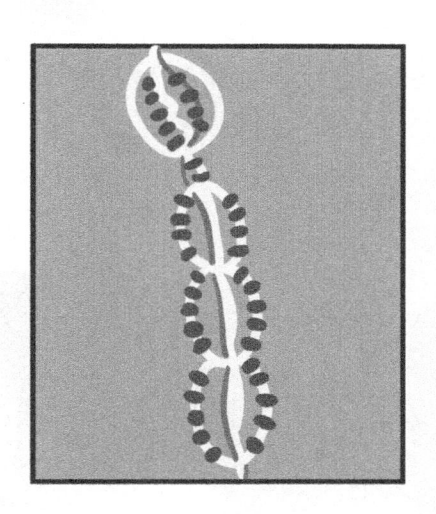

10. Now repeat steps 5 and 6 until you have 5 sets of spirals from the center point, thread on your clasp. Tie an overhand knot with each cord and glue well. Let dry completely. As this is the weakest point in the design, I advise trimming the excess cords and gluing again. Let dry.

Chapter 10
HOUSE PROJECTS

9. AMAZING MACRAMÉ CURTAIN

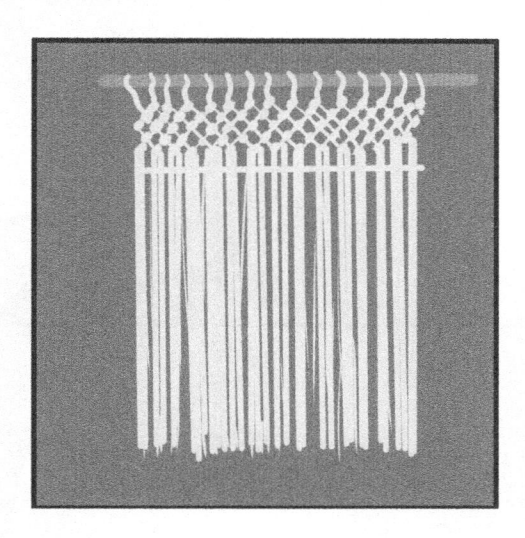

Macramé Curtains give your house the feel of that beach house look. You don't even have to add any trinkets or shells—but you can if you want to. Anyway, here's a great macramé Curtain that you can make!

Materials

- **Laundry rope (or any kind of rope/ the cord you want)**
- **Curtain rod**
- **Scissors**
- **Pins**
- **Lighter**
- **Tape**

Instructions

1. Tie four strands together and secure the top knots with pins so they could hold the structure down.

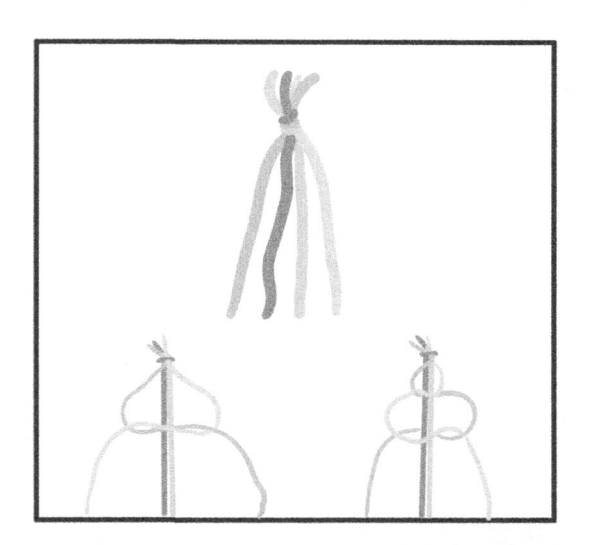

2. Take the strand on the outer right part and let it cross over to the left side by means of passing it through the middle. Tightly pull the strings together and reverse.

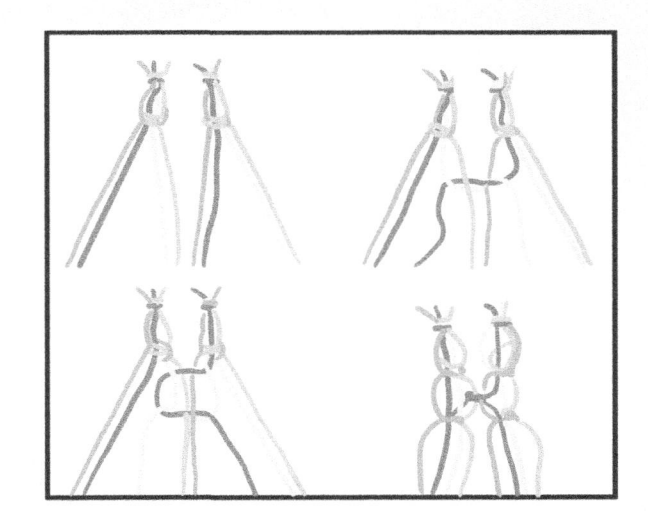

PAGE 91

3. Repeat crossing the thread over four more times for the thread you now have in front of you. Take the strand on the outer left and let it pass through the middle, and then take the right and let it cross over the left side. Repeat as needed, then divide the group of strands to the left, and also to the right. Repeat until you reach the number of rows you want.

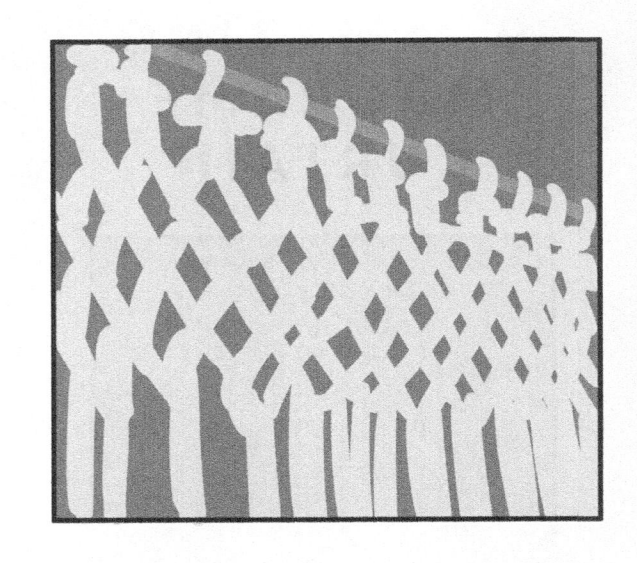

5. That's it, you can now use your new curtain!

4. You can now apply this to the ropes. Gather the number of ropes you want—10 to 14 is okay, or whatever fits the rod, with good spacing. Start knotting at the top of the curtain until you reach your desired length. You can burn or tape the ends to prevent them from unraveling.

Braid the ropes together to give them that dreamy, beachside effect, just like what you see below.

10. MACRAMÉ WALL ART

Adding a bit of macramé to your walls is always fun because it livens up space without making it cramped—or too overwhelming for your taste. It also looks beautiful without being too complicated to make. You can check it out below!

Materials

- **Large wooden beads**
- **Acrylic paint**
- **Painter's tape**
- **Scissors**
- **Paintbrush**
- **Wooden dowel**
- **70 yards rope**

Instructions

1. Attach the dowel to a wall. It's best to just use removable hooks so you won't have to drill anymore.

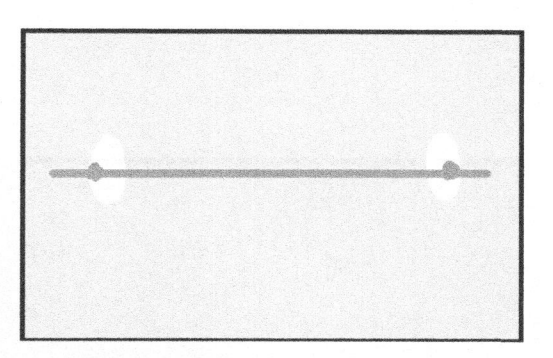

2. Cut the rope into 14 x 4 pieces, as well as 2 x 5 pieces. Use 5-yard pieces to bookend the dowel with. Continue doing this with the rest of the rope.

3. Then, start making double half-hitch knots and continue all the way through, like what's shown below.

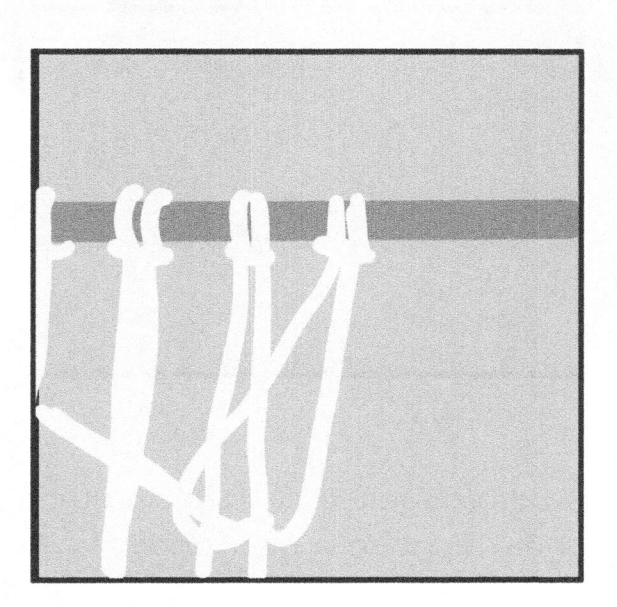

4. Once you get to the end of the dowel, tie the knots diagonally so that they wouldn't fall down or unravel in any way. You can also add the wooden beads any way you want, so you'd get the kind of décor that you need. Make sure to tie the knots after doing so.

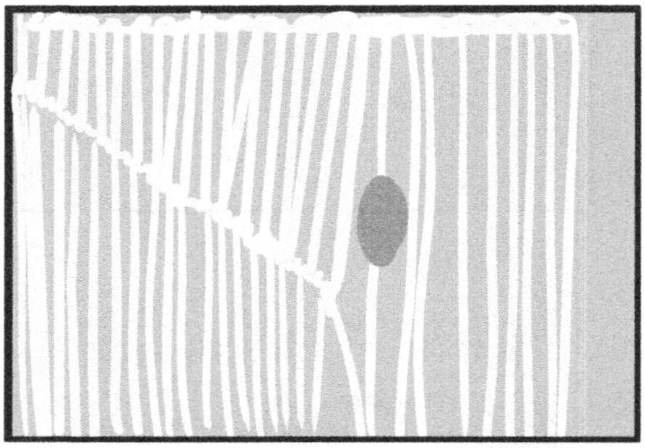

5. Use four ropes to make switch knots and keep the décor all the more secure. Tie around 8 of these.

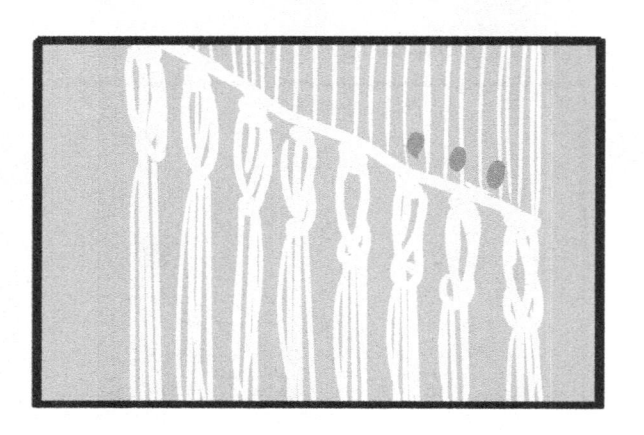

6. Add a double half hitch and then tie them diagonally once again.

7. Add more beads and then trim the ends of the rope.

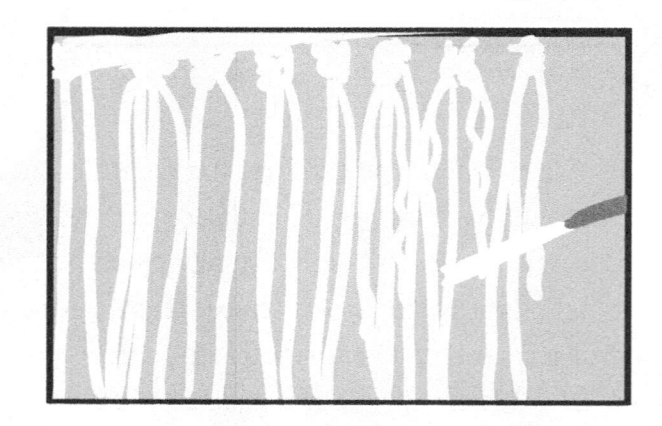

8. Once you have trimmed the rope, go ahead and add some paint to it. Summery or neon colors would be good.

PAGE 94

9. That's it! You now have your own macramé Wall Art!

PAGE 95

11. HANGING MACRAMÉ VASE

To add a dainty, elegant touch to your house, you could create a macramé Vase. With this one, you'll have to make use of basket stitches/knots—which you'll learn about below. It's also perfect for those who really love flowers—and want to add a touch of nature at home!

Materials

- **Masking tape**
- **Tape measure or ruler**
- **0 meters thick nylon cord**
- **Small round vase (with around 20 cm. diameter)**

Instructions

1. Cut eight cords measuring 3.5 yards or 3.2 meters each and set aside one of them. Cut a cord that measures 31.5 inches and set it aside, as well. Then, cut one cord that measures 55 inches.

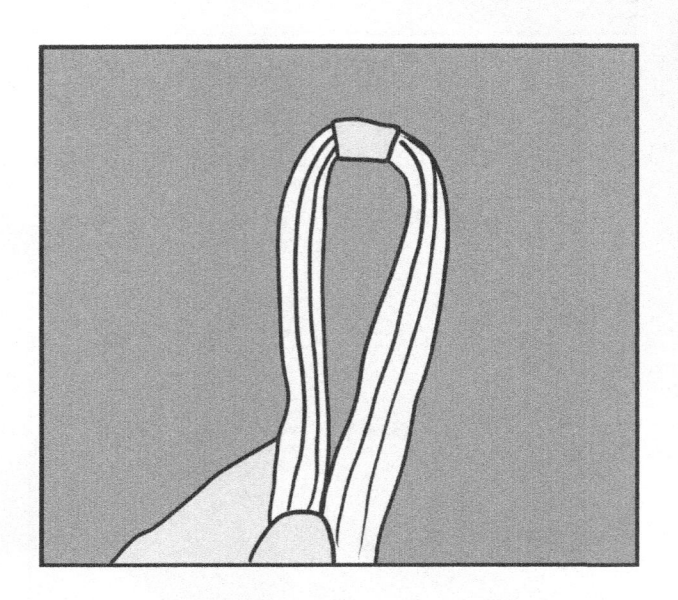

2. Now, group eight lengths of cord together—the ones you didn't set aside, of course, and mark the center with a piece of tape.

3. Wrap the cords by holding them down together and take around 80 cm. of it to make a tail—just like what you see below.

6. Divide the cords into groups of four and secure the ends with tape.

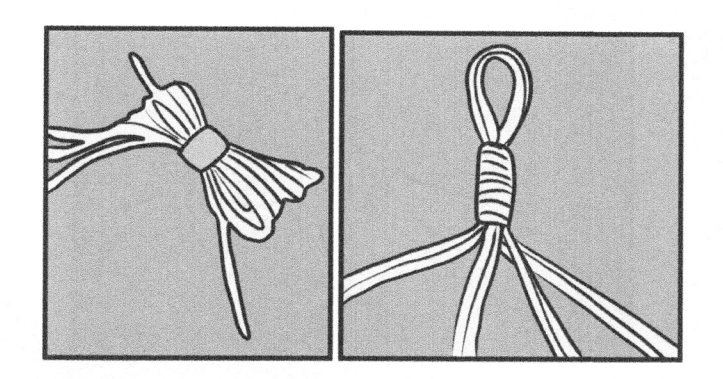

4. Wrap the cord around the back of the long part and make sure to keep your thumb on the tail. Then, wrap the cord around the main cord group. Make sure it is firm, but don't make it too tight. If you can make the loop bigger, that would be good, too.

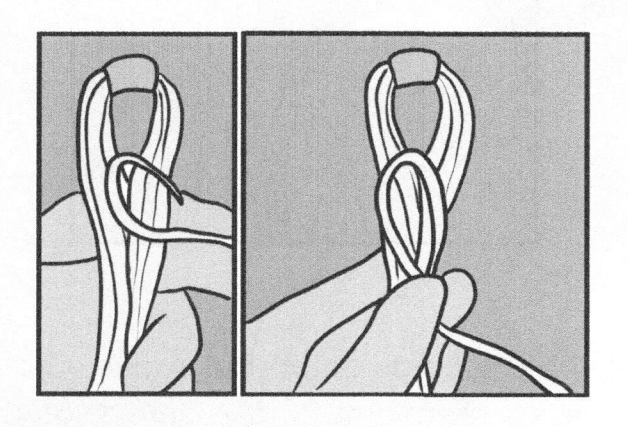

7. Get the group of cords that you have not used yet and make sure to measure 11.5 inches from the beginning—or on top. Do the overhand knot and get the cord on the left-hand side. Fold it over two of the cords and let it go under the cord on the right-hand side.

8. Fold the fourth cord and let it pass under the leftmost cord then up the loop of the first cord. Make sure to push it under the large knot so that it would be really firm.

5. Do it 13 more times through the loop and go and pull the tail down so the loop could soften up. Stop letting the cords overlap by pulling them whenever necessary and then cut both ends so they would not be seen anymore.

PAGE 97

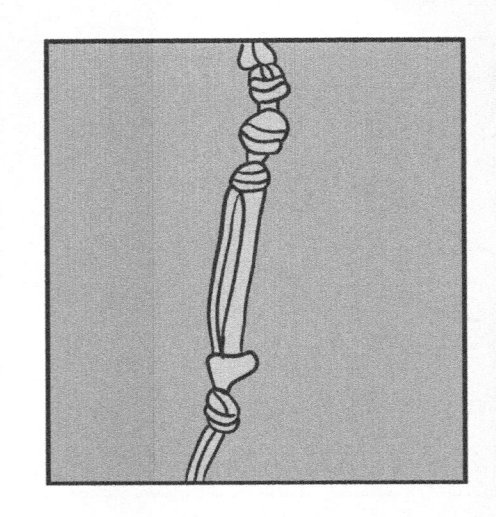

9. Make more half-hitches until you form more twists. Stop when you see that you have made around 12 of them and then repeat with the rest of the cords.

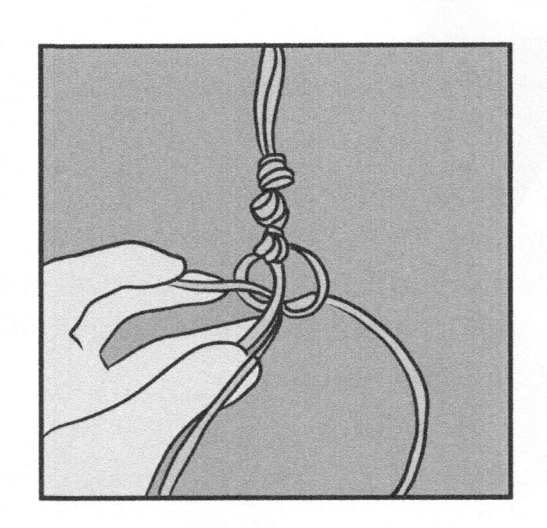

10. Now, it's time to make the basket for the vase. What you have to do here is measure 9 centimeters from your group of cords. Tie an overhand knot and make sure to mark with tape.

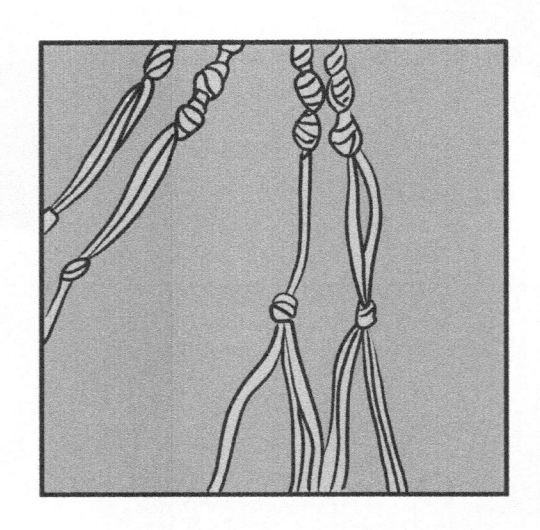

11. Let the two cord groups come together by laying them side by side.

12. Tie the cords down but make sure to keep them flat. Make sure that the knots won't overlap, or else you'd have a messy project—which isn't what you'd want to happen. Use two cords from the left as starting point and then bring the two cords on the right over the top of the loop. Loop them together under the bottom cords and then work them back up once more.

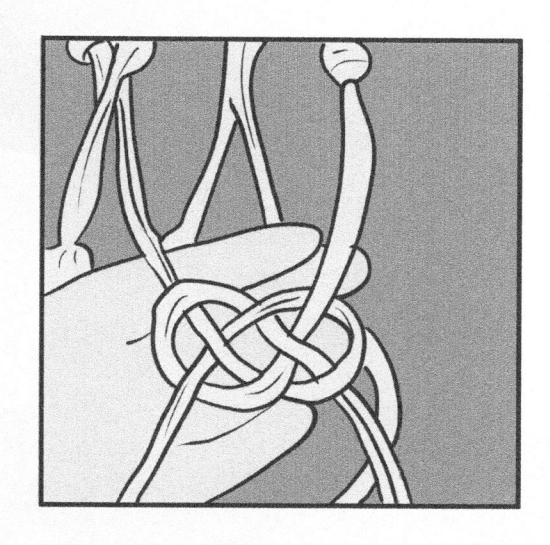

13. Now, find your original loop and thread the same cords behind them. Then, let them pass through the left-hand cords by making use of the loop once more.

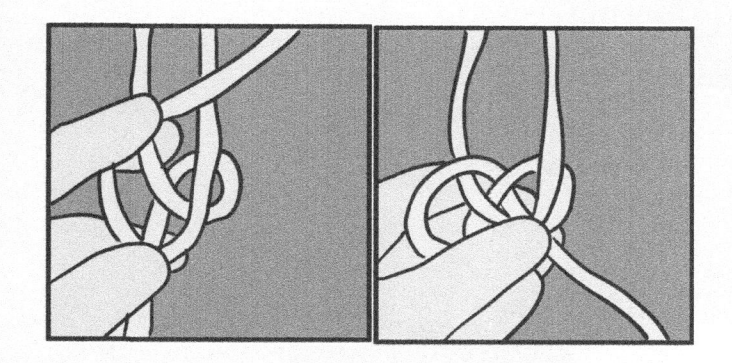

14. Let the knot move once you already have it in position. It should be around 3 inches or 7.5 cm. from the overhand knots. After doing so, make sure that you flatten the cords and let them sit on to each other until you have a firm knot on top. Keep dividing and letting cords come together.

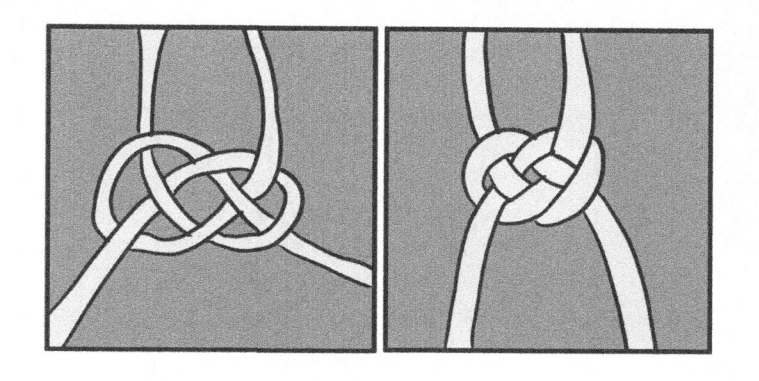

15. Get the cord on the left-hand side and let it go over the 2nd and 3rd cords before folding the fourth one under the first two cords. You'd then see a square knot forming between the 2nd and 3rd cords. You should then repeat the process on the right-hand side. Open the cord on the right side and let it go under the left-hand cord. Repeat this process thrice, then join the four-square knots that you have made by laying them out on a table.

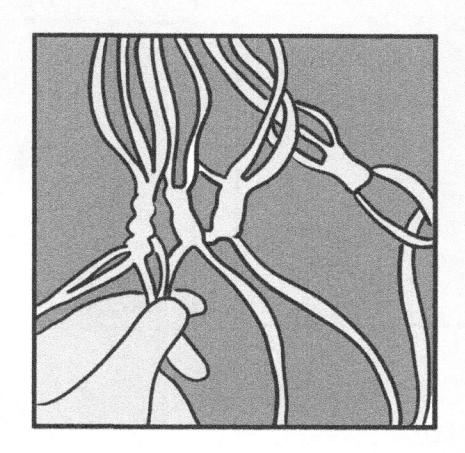

16. You'll then see that the cords have come together at the base. Now, you have to start wrapping the base by wrapping a 1.4-meter cord and wrap

PAGE 99

around 18 times.

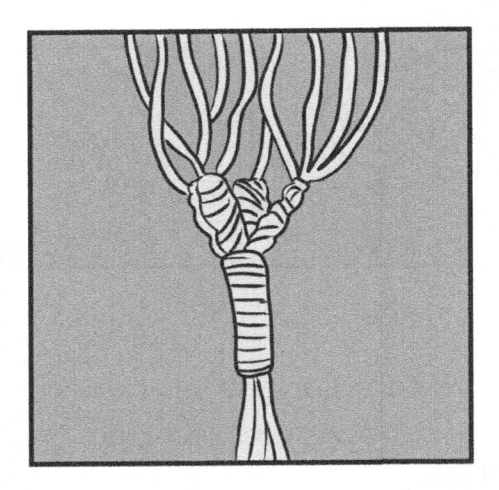

17. To finish, just cut the cords the way you want. It's okay if they're not of the same length so that there'd be variety—and they'd look prettier on your wall. Make sure to tie overhand knots at the end of each of them before placing the vase inside.

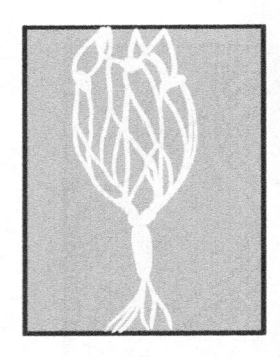

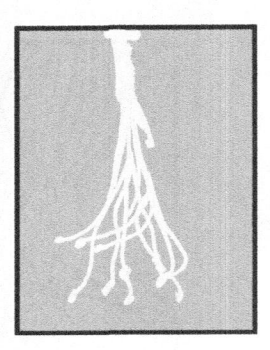

18. Enjoy your new hanging vase!

Chapter 11
EASY MACRAMÉ PROJECT FOR BEGINNERS

12. MASON JAR WALL HANGING

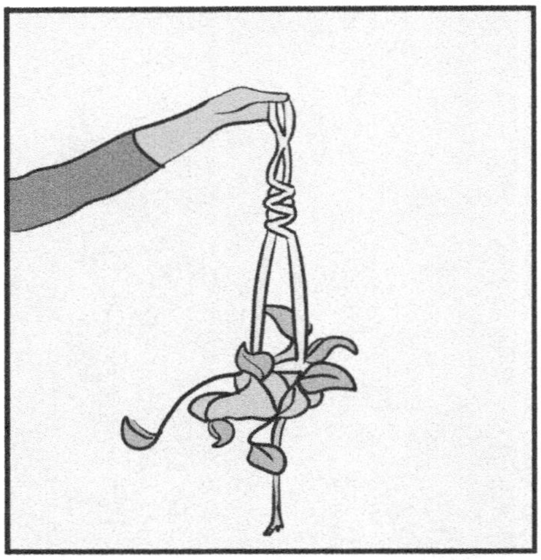

When it comes to art tools, Mason jars have remained popular. A mason jar can still come in handy from canning to sorting with hundreds of other innovative applications.

Materials
- **A mason jar**
- **Pair of scissors**
- **Macramé cords**
- **A plant**
- **Soil for the plant**

Notes: You will need a mason jar that is big enough to hold a plant with a little space to flourish. A pint-size or larger will most definitely be a suitable starting point. Choose your favorite form for your macramé cord, ranging from cotton to jute to polyester. It entirely depends on the type of look you prefer and how strong you would want the cord to be.

Instructions

1. Cut and knot

2. Cut the four lengths of the cord, each roughly about three yards wide. Fold them into half, then at the halfway point tie them all together, making a loop at the knot. That is where you would be hanging the final project from the ceiling or the wall.

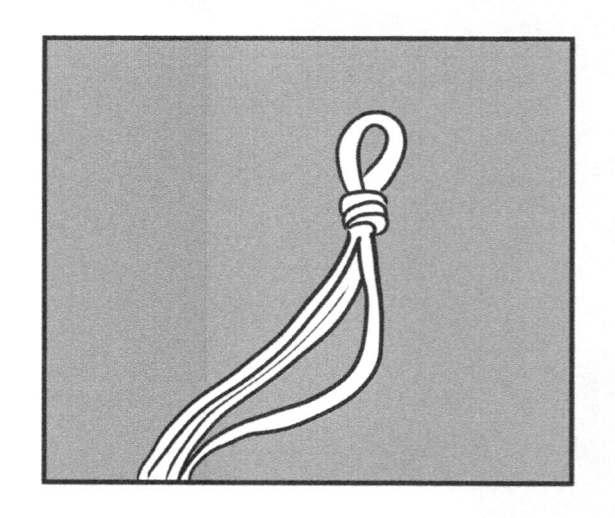

3. Split the cords into a pair of two cords each. Remember to leave almost four to five inches from the top of the knot and then knot the pairs together.

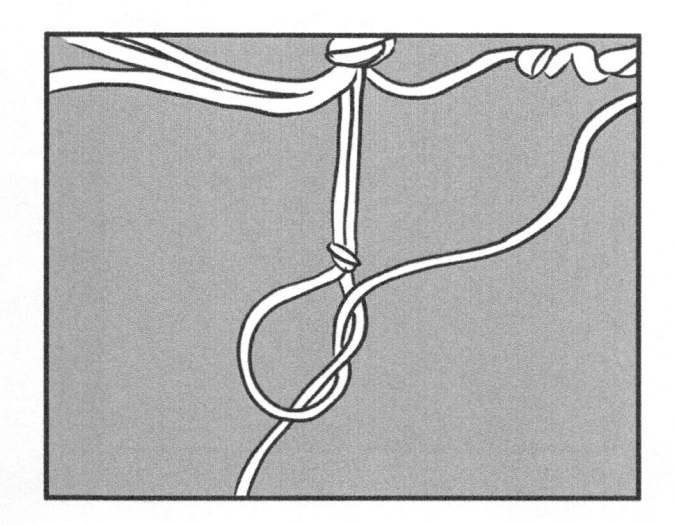

4. You'll now create a spiral knot pattern underneath each knotted set. Take a pair, then keep the taut right cord. Pass the left cord over the right, across the back and up, via the loop formed. Pull it tightly. Continue doing this cycle with the same cord, holding the initial right cord taut, and a form of the spiral knot should begin to appear. Continue the spiral knots until they are around four inches.

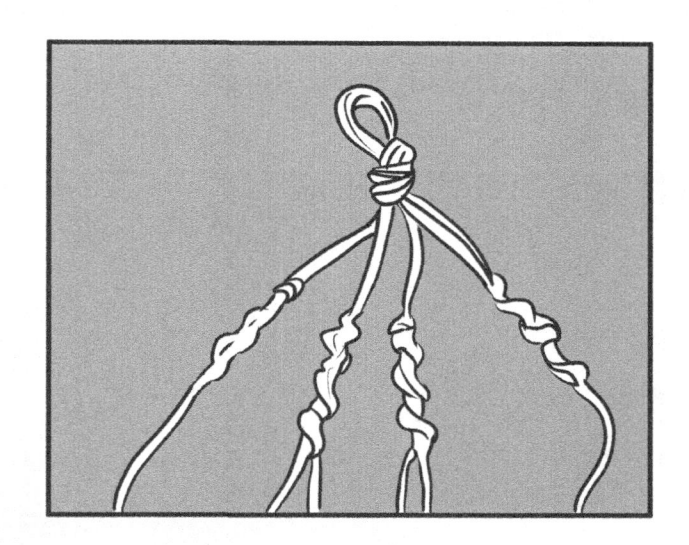

5. When all your pairs have been knotted spirally, leave around 12 inches in length on each set of cords. Create a knot for each pair of strings, at the mark of 12 inches.

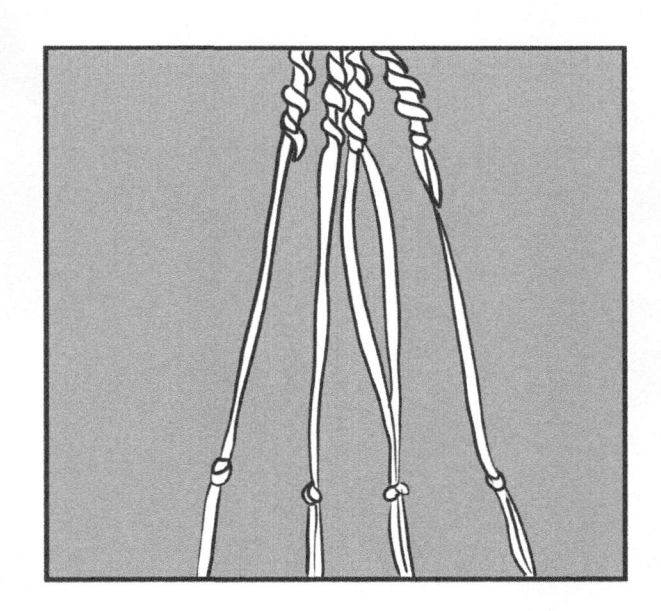

6. Set out all the pairs. Take the cord at right from the leftmost set and tie it with the left cord of the next nearest set, around 3 inches just below the tie. Continue the cycle, and switch

between pairs. Take the two exterior cords at the end and tie them together.

fit the Mason jar within the macramé hanger.

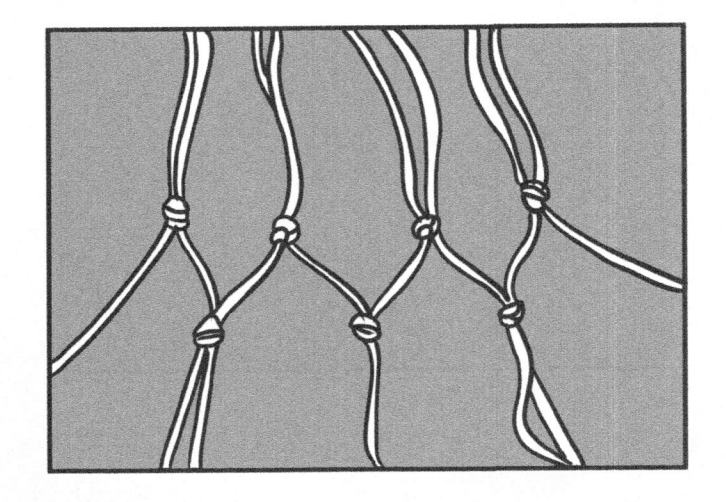

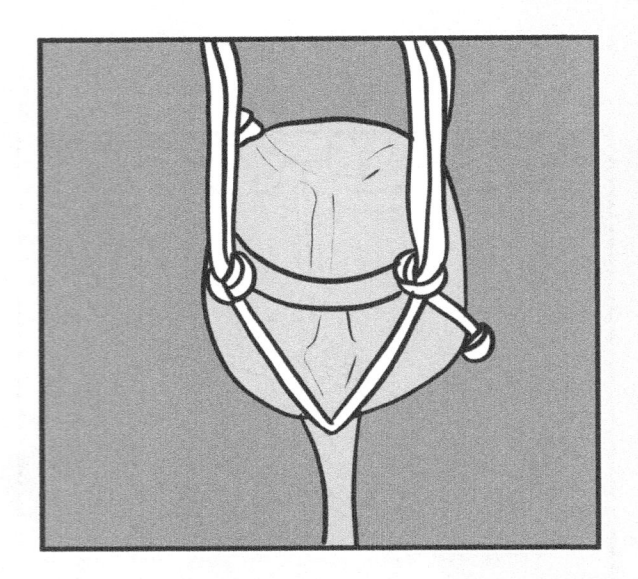

7. Around 3 inches below the range of knots tie all the cords together in a single big knot. Keep the hanging string for around 12 inches, then cut the ends.

9. Hang and enjoy!

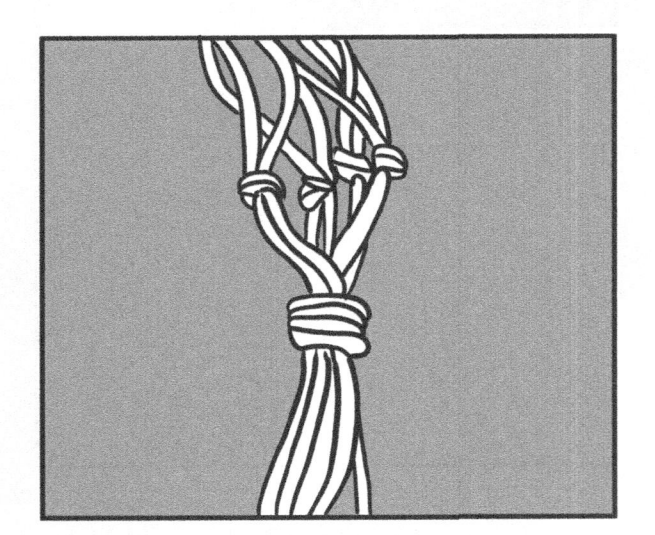

We can't see why you shouldn't create four or five of these cute little mini planters and liven up your workplace, room, or your kitchen area!

8. Place a mason jar, filling it with soil and the plant of your choice. It might be better to plant it before based on the scale of your greenery, and then

13. NET PRODUCE BAG DIY

I personally use these net bags a lot, and these are my favorite and so very useful! These are perfect for a trip to the lake, beach, or the farmer's market over the weekend. They hold whatever you need, but small crumbs may fall out. Particularly perfect for visits to the beach and the park.

The great news is that only two items are required to make it.

Materials
- **Macramé cords**
- **A pair of scissors**

Instructions

1. Cut the cord into 18 strands and make sure that each of them is 96 inches long. You're also going to cut one main cord that will knot all the others to around 80 inches in total. Fold in half the cord, and then loop it across the mainline.

2. Pull it tightly and keep going down the line. You would want them to be close together, within a ½ inch, so the holes on the bag are not too large. Move about 20 inches along the mainline.

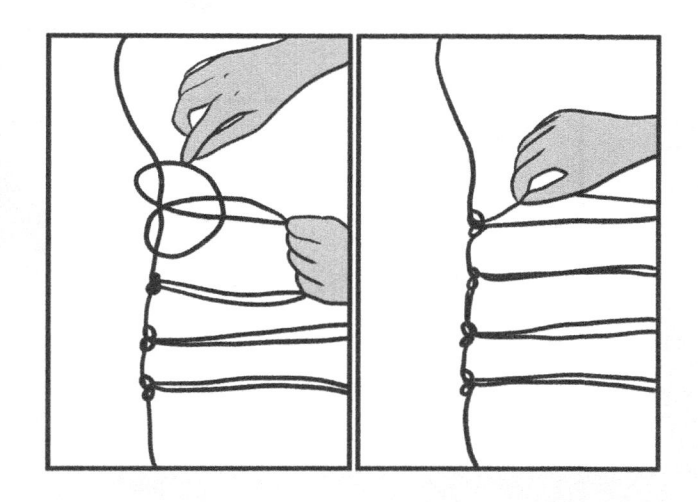

3. After you have reached the bottom line or gone all the way down the line, you will start collecting one piece from each of the knots to link them to the second layer of the knots, simultaneously leaving one string to be unattached.

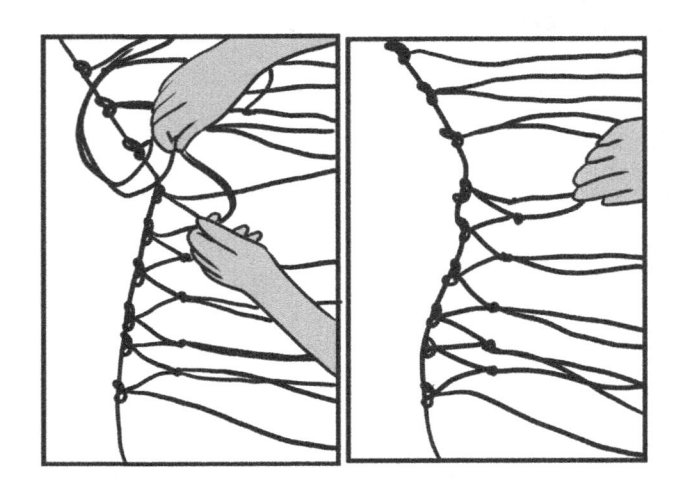

4. Repeat the same knotting process with the other side. You'll create the knots all the way to the bottom and the length of the bag.

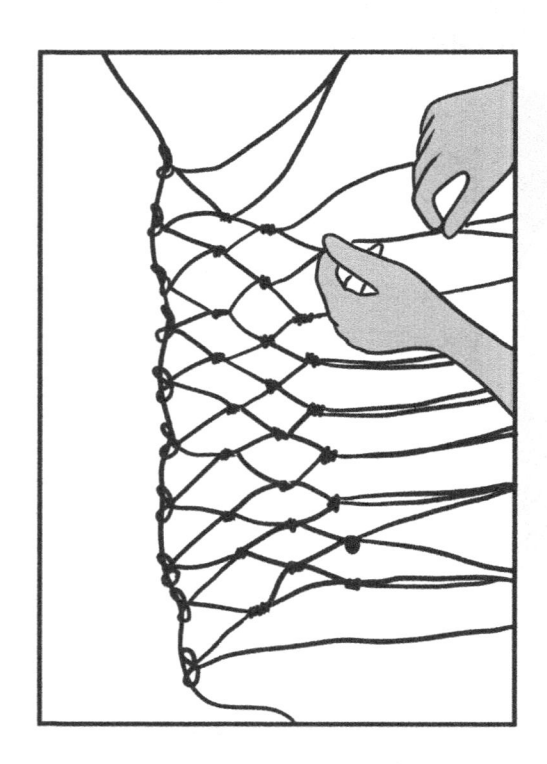

5. Fold the strand in half and take the extra strand that was left out in step 2.

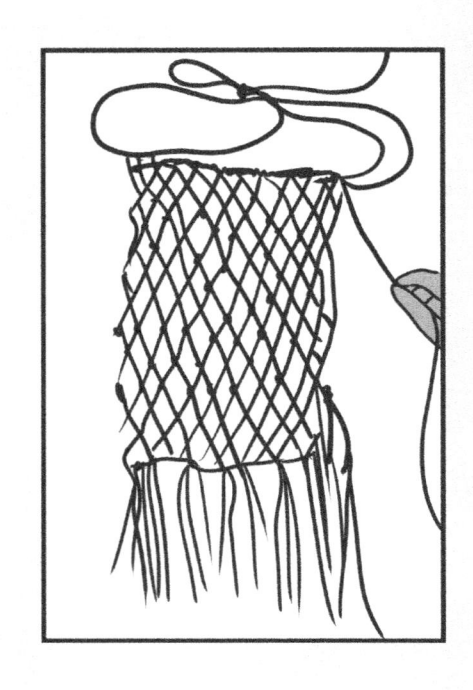

6. Then you will weave the strings that are unattached through the other two sides whilst making knots creating knots between each of the loops for connecting them together.

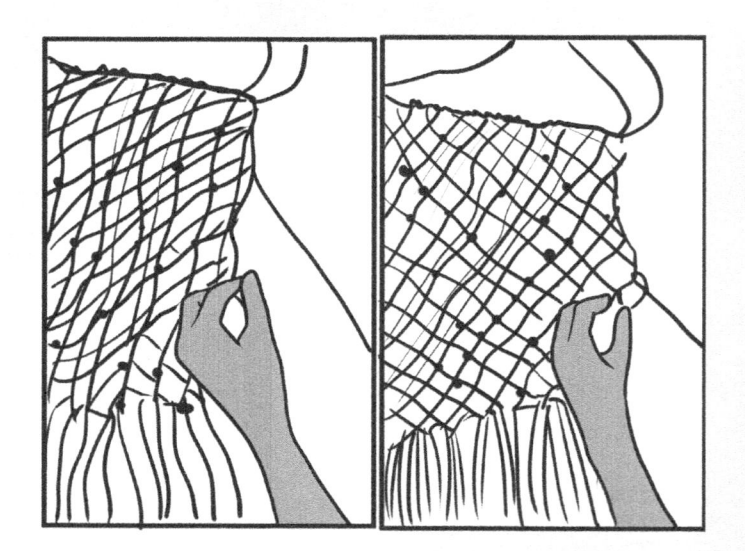

7. Take another piece of cord for tying a knot at the bottom in front as well as back also trimming the fringe's

PAGE 106

bottom. As shown in the picture below.

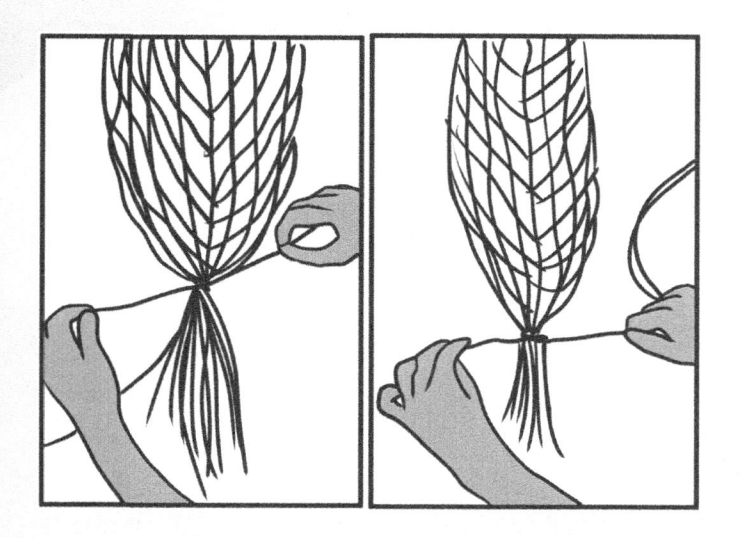

14. MACRAMÉ PLACEMATS DIY

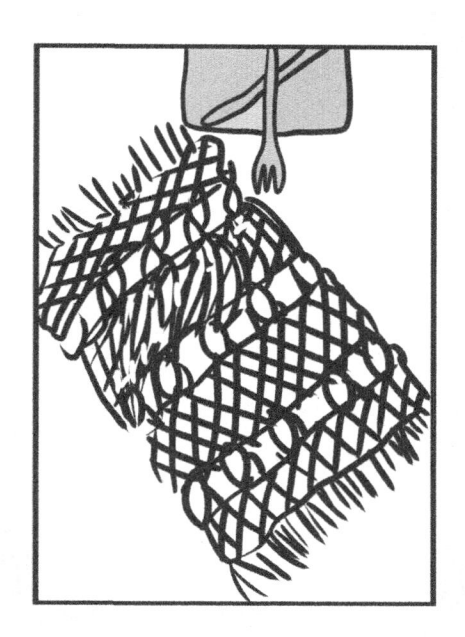

8. Take another extra cord from that of the mainline and attach a knot to it to the bottom for making a shoulder strap.

Materials

- Cords
- A hanger
- A pair of scissors

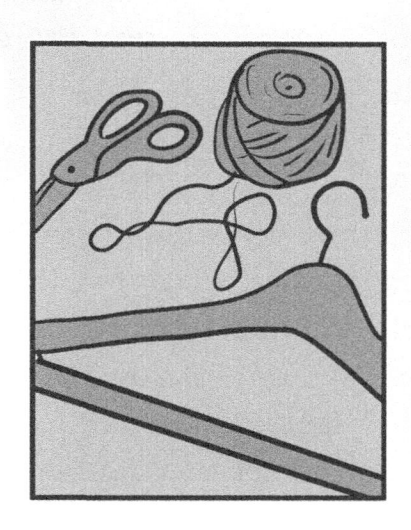

PAGE 107

Instructions

1. Begin by cutting 20 cords every 116 inches in total.

2. I am using Lark's Head Knots to tie each one of the 20 cords to the hanger.

3. Leave a space of around 1.5 inches and create a row of square knots from there, accompanied by an alternating row of square knots.

4. Continue this sequence until 5 rows of square knots are there.

5. Take 8 of the adjacent cords, then make one knot in the middle of the two cords. Each of these "center" cords will be used as the leader cord. On the diagonal to the left, one central cord will be worked on, and the other on the right. We are creating the shape of a diamond. Woot!

6. Taking the middle cord to the right, put it over the three cords to the right. Use double half-hitch knots to attach each of the 3 cords. Take the central cord on the left side and put it to the left of the three cords. Use double half-hitch knots to connect each of those three cords. You will have the shape of a triangle until you're finished!

7. Now—take those leader cords and put them back for a minute. You must create a square knot in the triangle center. You'll get four instead of just two middle cords!

8. Continue the process of creating the diamond shape using double hitch knots whilst working them towards the middle.

9. When the rows of the two double hitch knots begin to meet in the center, then tie a small knot. This will help to tighten it.

10. This means we are back to making 5 rows of square knots!

11. Repeat this process in the same pattern at least 5 times. (5 rows of square ties, a double half hitch diamond, and a square knot in the center)

12. When your pattern is finished, cut off the placemat from the hanger, just below the head knots of the lark.

13. Hang your placemat over your hanger evenly or fold it in two. Trim the other half of the placemat until it's even with the first side you have cut off.

15. TASSEL AND MACRAMÉ KEY CHAINS

Materials

- 3 /16 inches piping cotton cord
- A key ring
- Yarn or an embroidery floss
- A wooden bead
- A pair of scissors

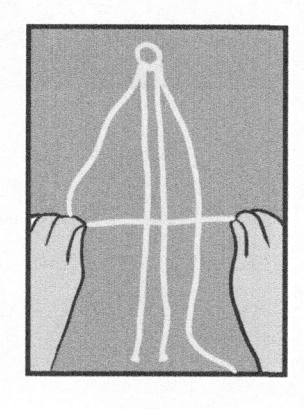

Instructions

1. To start with, connect both cords to the key ring using a basic lark's head knot (also recognized as a cow hitch), each with 1/3 length inside and 2/3 length outside.

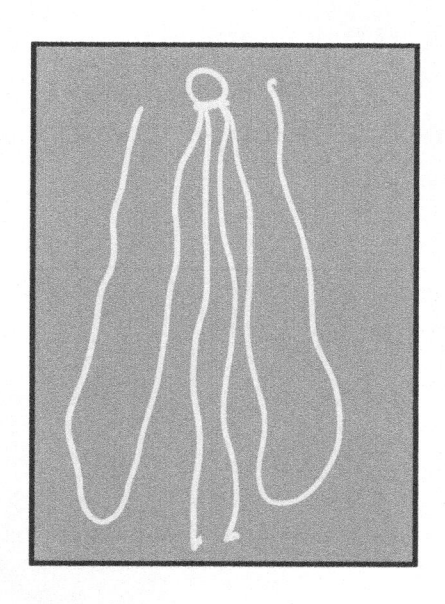

2. Now create a half square knot: Cross the left cord on the outside loosely over the two middle cords, just below the outside right cord to form a shape of 4.

3. Put the right outer chord under both center-cords and then to the through the loop that is created by the outer left cord.

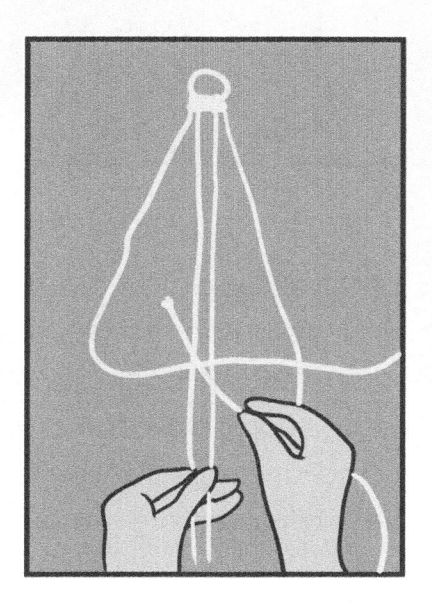

PAGE 109

4. Take out all outer cords and tighten until the knot snugly rests beside the knots on the top. Pull cords straight in the middle.

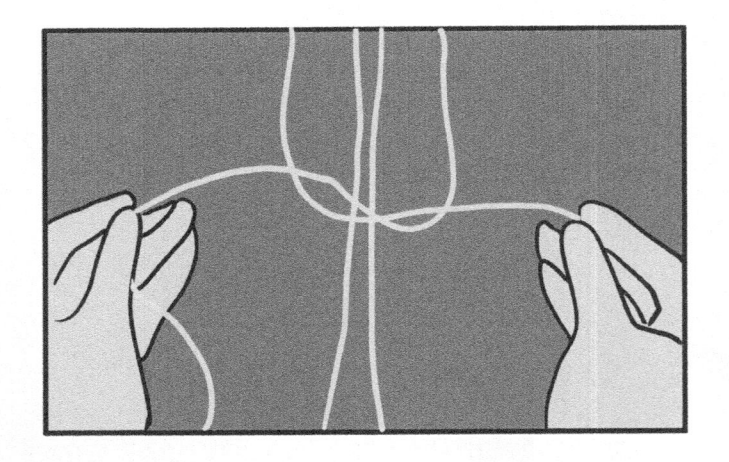

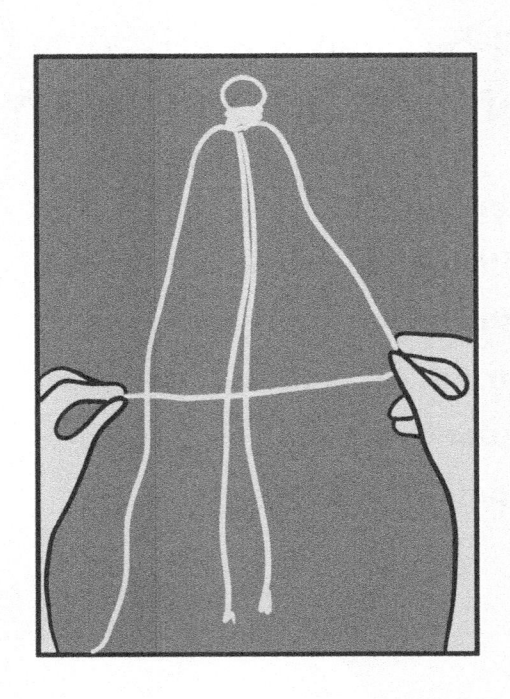

6. Put the left outer chord beneath all middle cables, and into the loop created by the right cord on the outside.

5. You will complete a full square knot for the next step by doing the same thing, except it would be backward: Pass the right outer cord over the two middle cords, and underneath the outer cord to build a backward 4 shape.

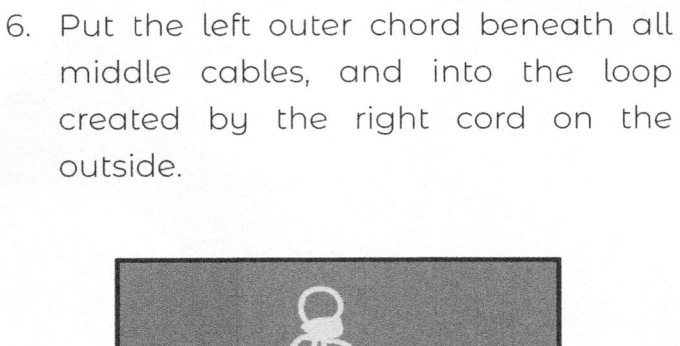

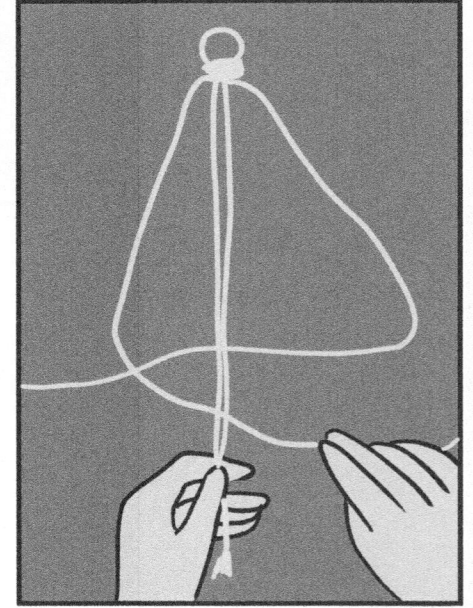

7. Take out all exterior cords and stretch till the knot is smooth with the first knot. Now you have a perfect square knot completed.

9. Then take a wooden bead and thread the 2 center cords through it.

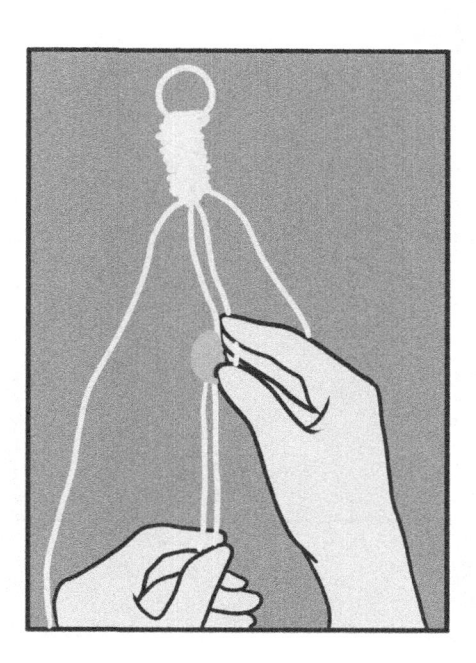

10. Take the left cord on the outside and form another half-square knot, then pull it slowly against the bead.

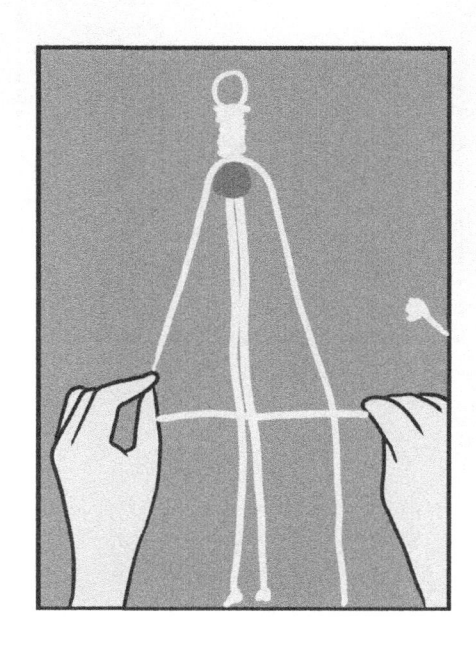

8. Repeat the same process from steps 2 to 7 to make 5 square knots.

PAGE 111

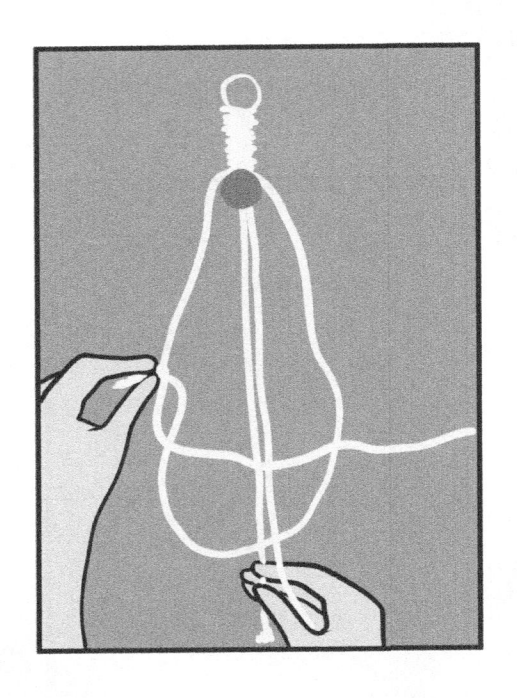

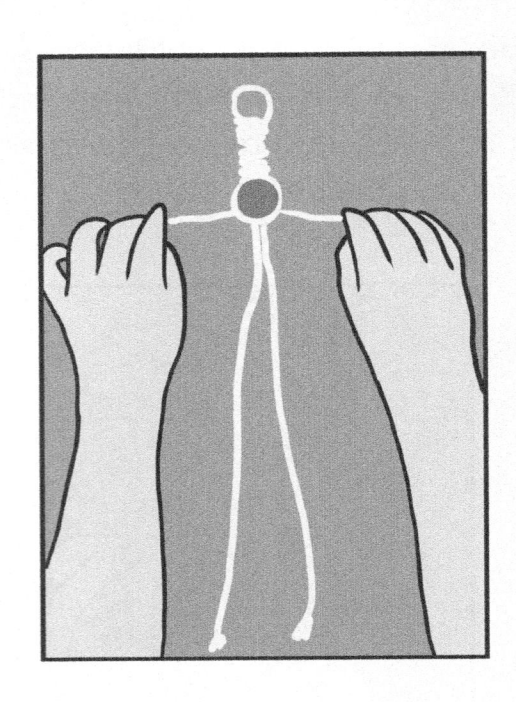

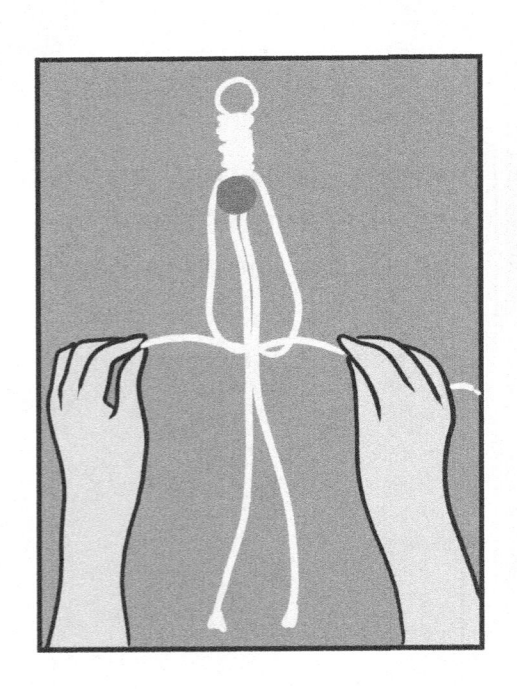

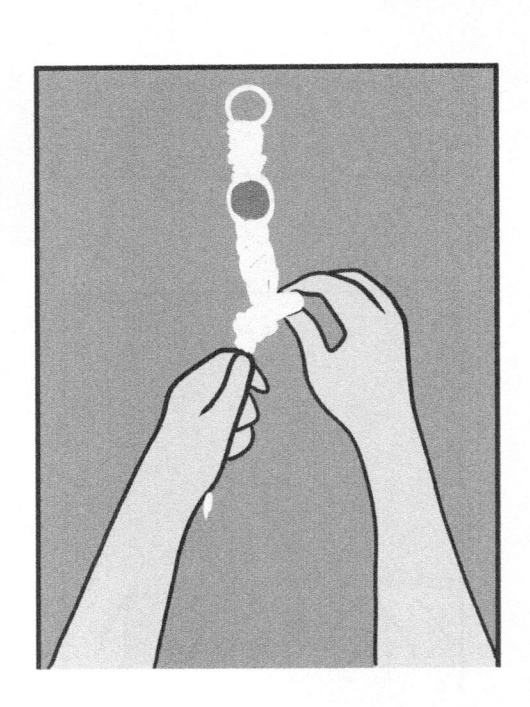

11. For the completion of the keychain, you should loop all four cords in an easy handed knot.

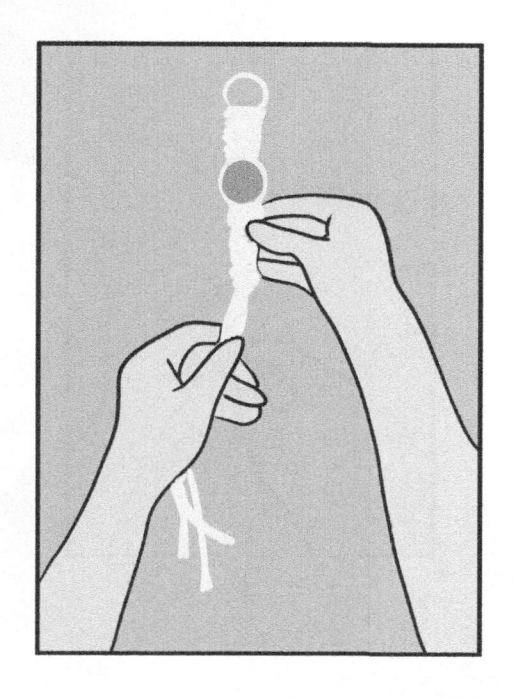

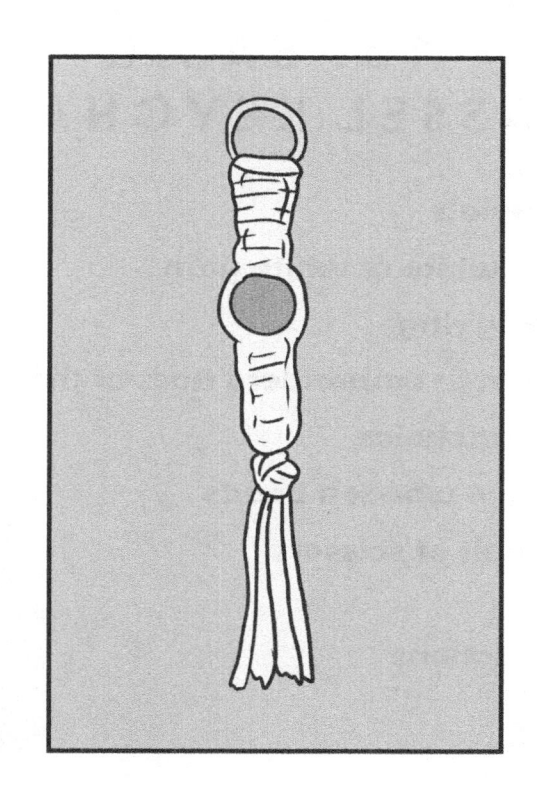

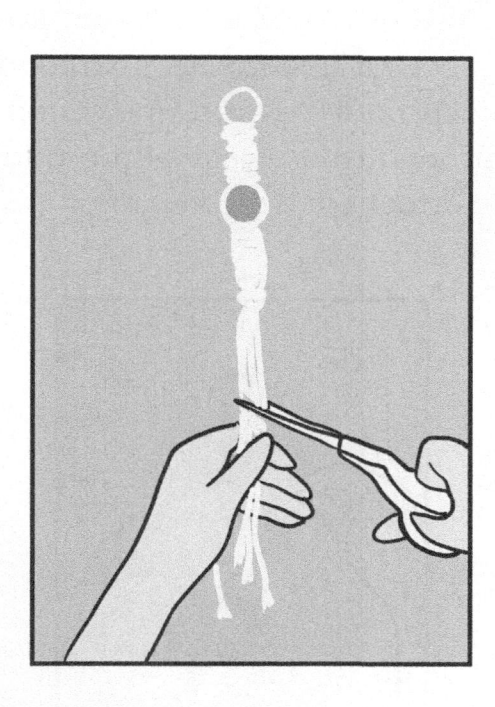

12. In the last step, all you need to do is trim the edges of the keychain, and it's good to go!

PAGE 113

16. BASIC TASSEL KEYCHAIN

Materials

- **Off white or white yarn**
- **1 key ring**
- **Yarn or embroidery floss of the color of your choice**
- **2 to 4 wooden beads**
- **A pair of scissors**

Instructions

1. To begin, by using a lark's head knot (which is also called a cow hitch knot), attach a yarn of 20 inches in length to the key ring.

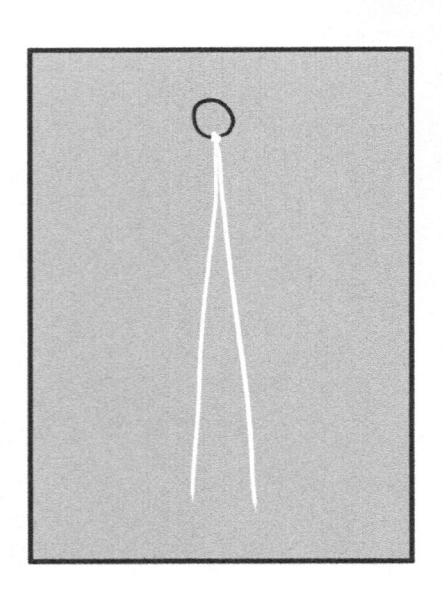

2. Both ends of the year should be threaded into the wooden beads.

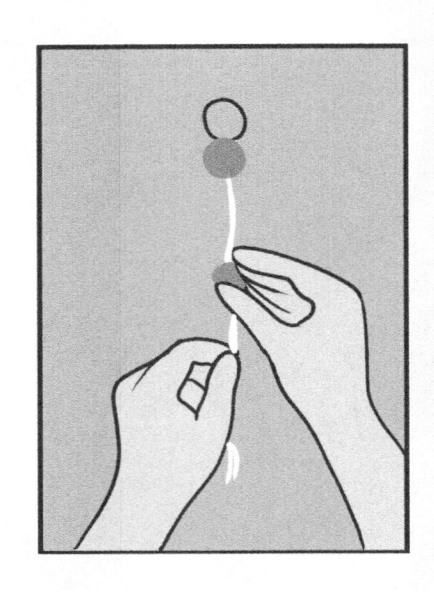

3. You should cut almost 20 pieces of yarn, which are twice the length of the tassel that you fancy. Hold them in a bunch, which is even, and center them between two pieces of the yarn that are attached to the key ring.

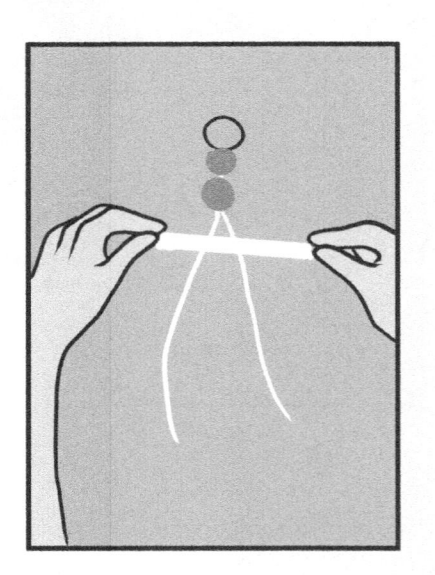

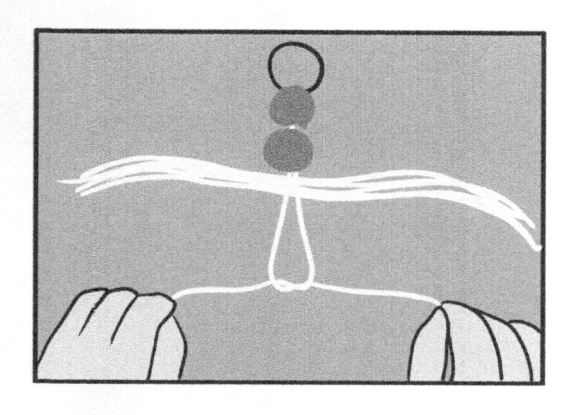

4. Knot the two pieces of the yarn against the bunch of yarn in a basic knot.

5. Ensure that all the beads are tight, and the tassel is cut in two lengths, which are relatively equal. Remove the knot to fasten, and then continue to tie another knot.

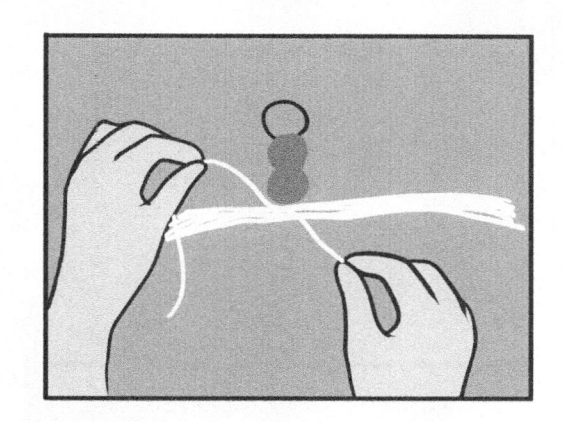

6. The ends of the tassel should be folded and smoothen together.

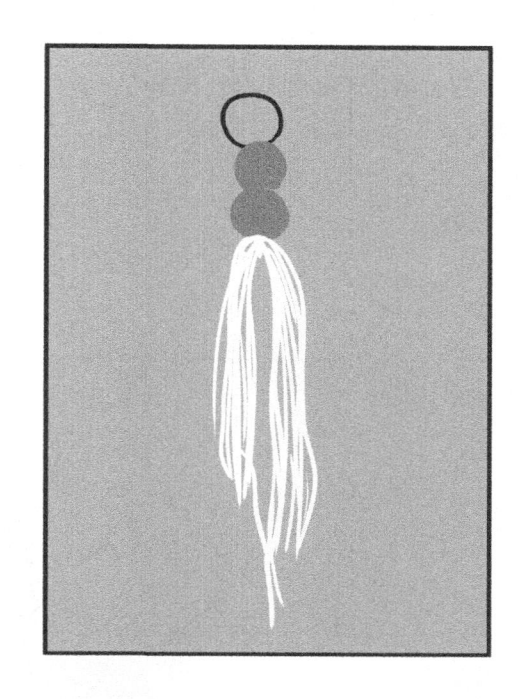

7. You are using a threaded embroidery skein to create the tassel's neck. With the full skein to the right, pull the loose end around, under, and then around the tassel where you want to begin the neck's top. Fold it up and down to create a loop.

8. Wrap the thread straight around the tassel, using the skein end, going forward as you head through the ends. Once your neck is to your desired length, wrap it back up towards the loop.

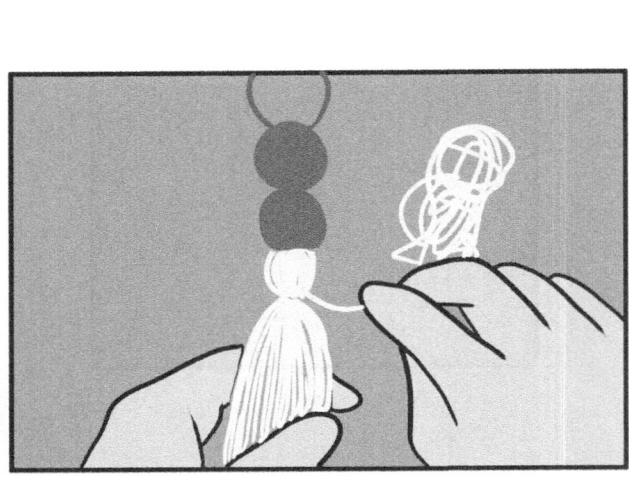

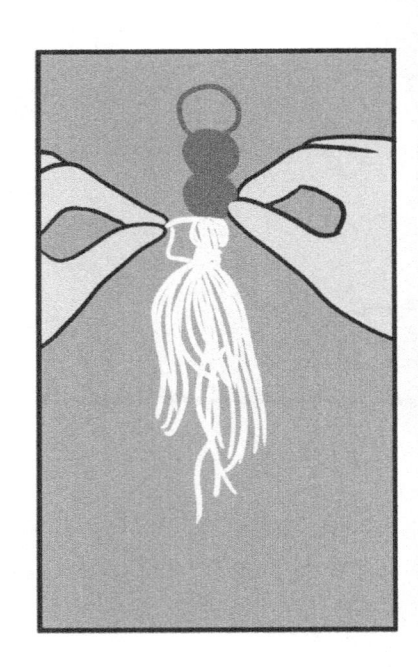

9. Trim the ends should be poked through the loop created.

10. Pull the bottom and the top in opposite directions.

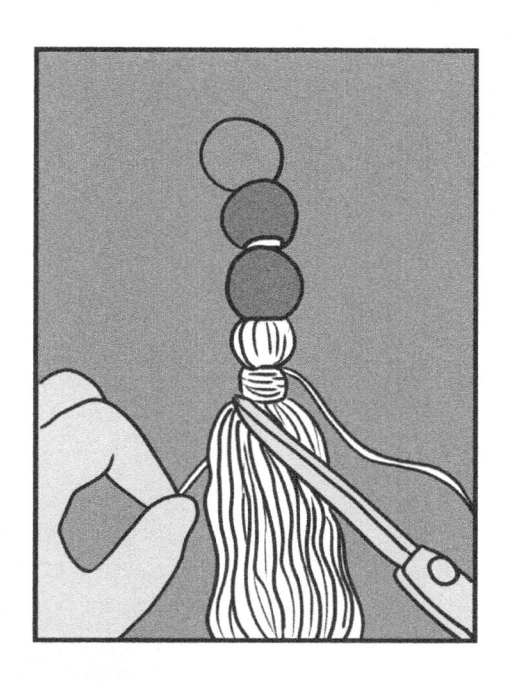

11. Pull it tight till the loop fades into the created neck.

12. Trim embroidery thread ends.

13. And lastly, trim the ends of the tassel for an even look.

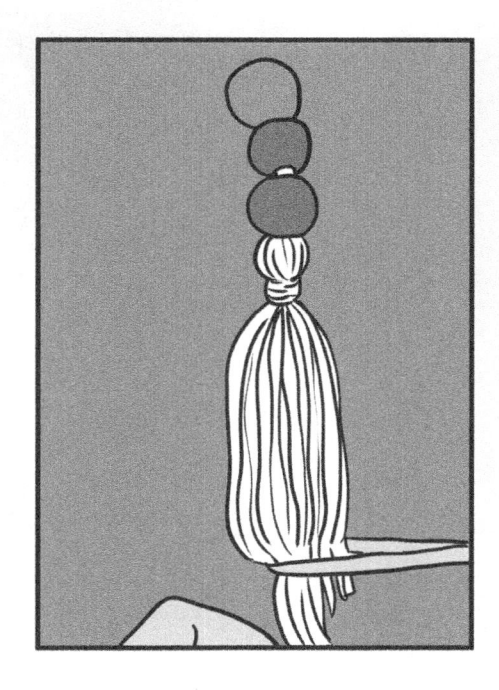

PAGE 117

Chapter 12
ACCESSORIES

17. MACRAMÉ TIE-DYE NECKLACE

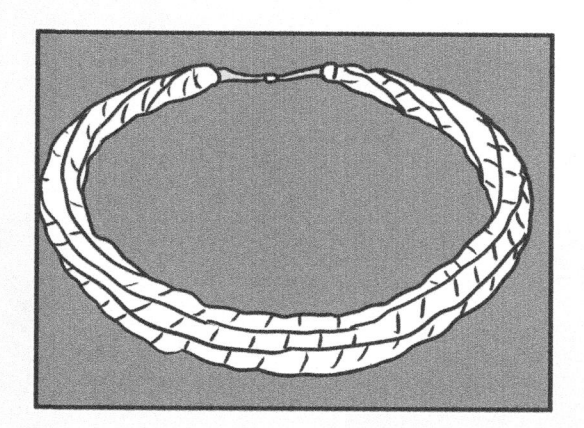

This one is knotted tightly, which gives it the effect that it is strong—but still elegant. This is a good project to craft—you would enjoy the act of making it, and wearing it, as well!

Materials

- **1 pack laundry rope**
- **Tulip One-Step Dye**
- **Fabric glue**
- **Candle**
- **Jump rings**
- **Lobster clasp**

Instructions

1. Tie the rope using crown knots.

2. After tying, place the knotted rope inside the One-Step Dye pack (you could get this in most stores) and let it sit and dry overnight.

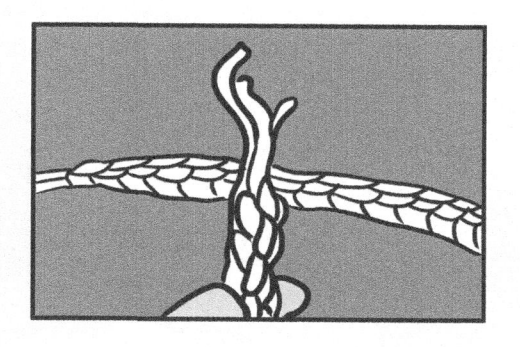

3. Upon taking it out, leave it for a few hours and then secure the end of the knot with fabric glue mixed with a bit of water.

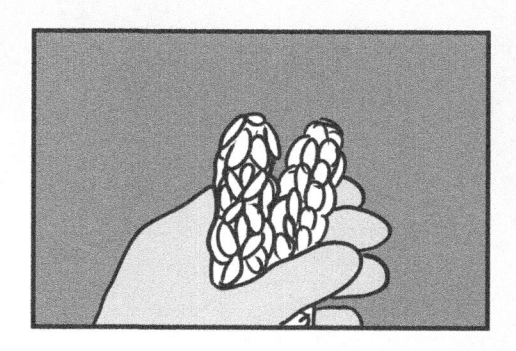

4. Trim the ends off and burn off the ends with wax from the candle.

PAGE 119

5. Add jump rings to the end and secure with a lobster clasp.

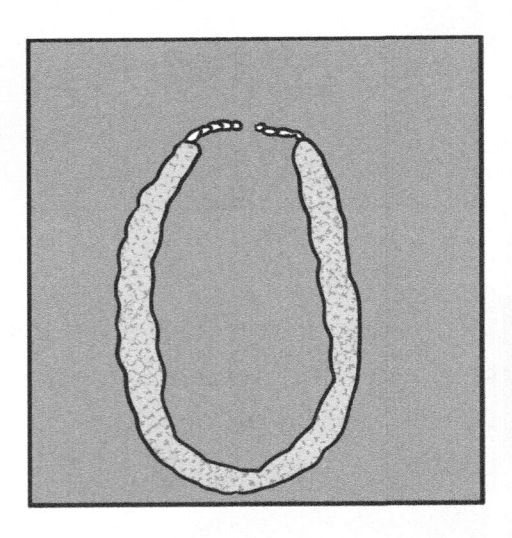

6. Enjoy your tie-dye necklace!

18. MACRAMÉ WATCH STRAND

If you are looking for ways to spice up your wristwatch, well, now's your chance! Make use of this macramé watch strand pattern and you will get what you want!

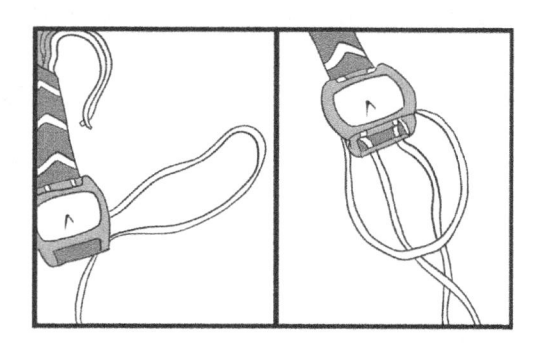

Materials

- Jump rings
- Closure
- 2 mm. crimp ends (you can choose another size, depending on your preferences)
- Embroidery or craft floss
- Watch with posts

Instructions

1. Choose your types of floss, as well as their colors. Take at least 10 long strands for each side of the watch.

2. Lash each floss onto the bar/posts of the watch and thread like you would a regular macramé bracelet or necklace.

3. Braid the ends tightly if you want to make them more stylish and cut the ends. Burn with a lighter to secure before placing jump rings and closure.

4. Use and enjoy!

PAGE 121

19. MACRAMÉ GEM NECKLACE

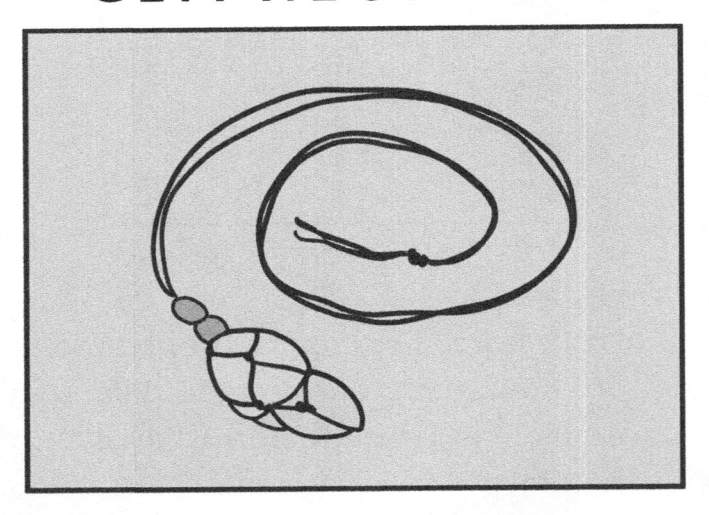

This one has that enchanting, beautiful feel! Aside from knots, it makes use of gemstones that could really spruce up your look! Surely, it's one necklace you'd love to wear repeatedly!

Materials

- **Your choice of gemstones**
- **Beads**
- **Crocheted or waxed cotton**
- **Water**
- **Glue**

Instructions

1. Get four equal lengths of cotton—this depends on how long you want the necklace to be.

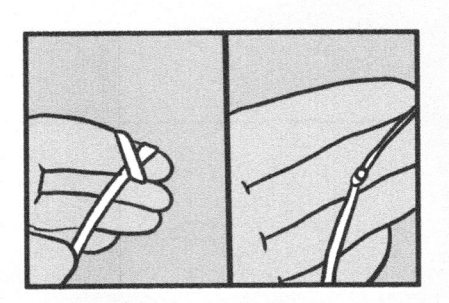

2. Tie a base knot as you hold the four cotton lengths. Once you do this, you'd notice that you'd have eight pieces of cotton lengths with you. What you should do is separate them into twos and tie a knot in each of those pairs before you start knotting with the square knot.

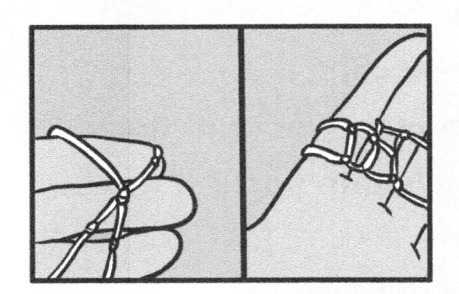

3. Tie individual strands of the cotton to the length next to it. Make sure you see some depth before stringing any gemstones along and make sure to knot before and after adding the gemstones to keep them secure.

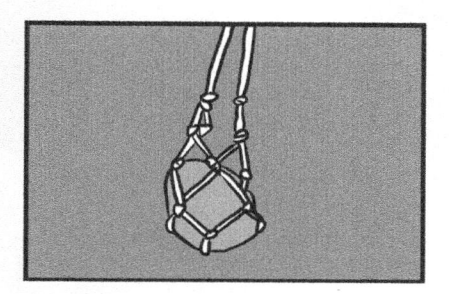

4. Take four of the strands in your hand and tie a knot on the top side of the bag. Tie strands until you reach the length and look you want.

5. Knot the ends to avoid spooling and use water with glue to keep it more secure.

20. YARN TWISTED NECKLACE

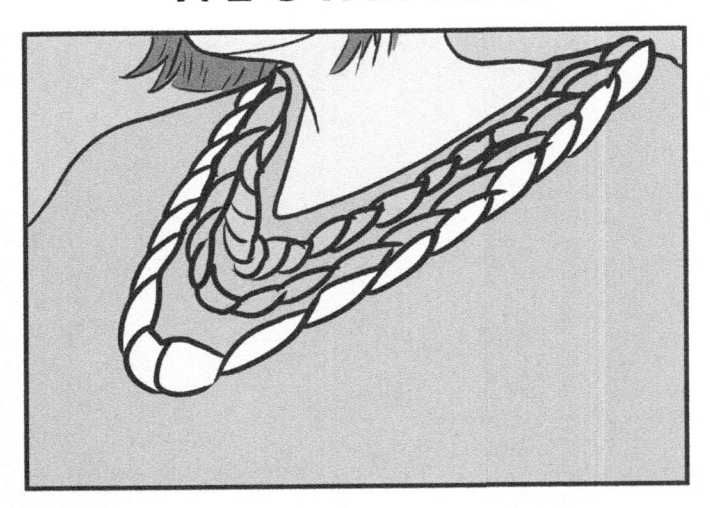

This one is quite simple as you can use any kind of yarn that you want, especially thick or worsted ones to give your projects more flair and to make them modest—but wearable!

Materials

- **Yarn in various colors**
- **Water**
- **Glue**

Instructions

1. Cut two to four pieces of yarn—it's up to you how much you want.

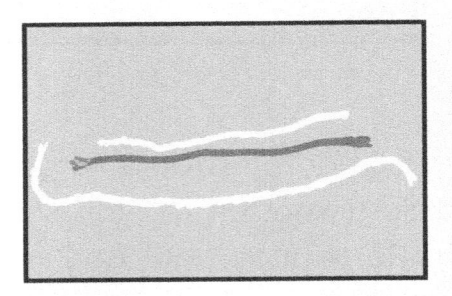

2. Start braiding, and knot using the square knot. Make sure that you secure the pieces of yarn together.

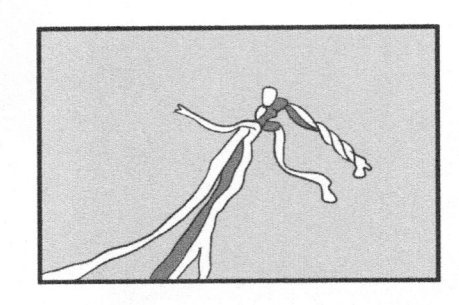

3. Knot until your desired length, then secure the piece with a mix of glue and water at the ends.

Conclusion

Macramé is a very interesting kind of art that is easy to learn yet can be used in many ways depending on the skill level. It combines loops, knots, and even braiding to create pieces that vary from simple bracelets to complex wall hangings. It's amazing how many projects you can make just from this one craft.

Macramé is a craft that can be traced back to ancient Egypt. Artisans learned how to create fabric garlands for adults and children by combining loops, knots, and braiding to create pieces that varied from simple bracelets to complex wall hangings. The term macramé was first coined in the 18th century.

Macramé takes a lot of practice and patience to become good at. However, it is worth the time and effort to learn for the many benefits it has to offer. Many people turn to macramé because they enjoy the challenge.

Macramé is also very flexible in terms of what it can be used for. Most of its creations are for decorating, but some people also use macramé to relax and let go of stress and tension. Others use macramé as a hobby. No matter how you use macramé it's sure to be beneficial and rewarding.

The type of macramé that you do will determine your results. The easier the pattern is to make, the less time it should take you. However, if you want something more intricate and time-consuming, feel free to choose a more difficult pattern.

Macramé is inexpensive when compared to other forms of art because all you need to create it are supplies like thread, fabric, and anchors which are very accessible at almost any sewing store. While you may want to invest in more decorative materials, the basic five supplies can be used for many different types of macramé projects.

Macramé is also very easy to learn. It does not take a lot of practice to get good at creating items with it because most of the time is spent creating your pattern. Once you've mastered the art of macramé, you're sure to enjoy the benefits.

Arts and crafts have always been popular hobbies around the world that people of all ages and abilities can enjoy. It's amazing how many projects you can make just from this one craft. This art form has been around for centuries because it's so simple yet versatile in how it can be used.

The craft is also environmentally friendly. While most forms of macramé are handmade, this alternative allows you to create without causing damage to the environment or yourself.

Macramé is also something that can be done in a small amount of space. It does not require a lot of space or large supplies to create, so it's a great craft to do when you have limited resources.

Macramé does not require you to have any special talents to create amazing things, so it can be enjoyed by many kinds of people. Macramé will take some time to learn if you want results that are more aesthetically pleasing and intricate.

I hope you enjoyed learning more about macramé for beginners and decide to take the time to try it yourself. Macramé is great for relaxing or a hobby, and once you get the hang of it you'll be eager to continue creating new pieces.

Made in the USA
Monee, IL
14 November 2022